MAKING THE WRITING AND RESEARCH CONNECTION WITH THE I-SEARCH PROCESS

A How-To-Do-It Manual

Marilyn Z. Joyce
Julie I. Tallman

*HOW-TO-DO-IT MANUALS
FOR LIBRARIANS*

NUMBER 62

NEAL-SCHUMAN PUBLISHERS, INC.
New York, London

Published by Neal-Schuman Publishers, Inc.
100 Varick Street
New York, NY 10013

Printed and bound in the United States of America.

Library of Congress Cataloging-in-Publication Data

Joyce, Marilyn Z.
    Making the writing and research connection with the I-search process : a how-to-do-it manual for teachers and school librarians / by Marilyn Z. Joyce, Julie I. Tallman.
        p. cm.—(How-to-do-it manuals for librarians ; no. 62)
    Includes bibliographical references and index.
    ISBN 1-55570-252-X (alk. paper)
    1. Library orientation for high school students. 2. Information retrieval—Study and teaching (Secondary) 3. Report writing—Study and teaching (Secondary) 4. Critical thinking—Study and teaching (Secondary) 5. Library orientation for high school students—Maine. 6. Information retrieval—Study and teaching (Secondary)—Maine. 7. Report writing—Study and teaching (Secondary)—Maine. 8. Critical thinking—Study and teaching (Secondary)—Maine. I. Tallman, Julie I., 1944– . II. Title. III. Series: How-to-do-it manuals for libraries ; no. 62.
Z711.2.J8   1996
025.5'678223—dc20   95-47717

To our students and our colleagues, who have made this book possible through their patience and willingness to share their journeys.

CONTENTS

PREFACE

Making the Writing and Research Connection with the I-Search Process: A How-to-Do-It Manual is a labor of love. The I-Search is an approach to research that uses the power of student interests, builds a personal understanding of the research process, and encourages stronger student writing. Originally developed by a college professor for his freshmen composition students, the I-Search is adaptable for use as a beginning research experience at the third grade level or a sophisticated search at the graduate level.

From the media specialist and media specialist educator perspective, we are teachers of and believers in the I-Search process as the best tool we have found for connecting students effectively to the research process. We delight in our students' personal triumphs and growth in their research process, their newfound belief in their writing ability, and their joy in discovering research as a means to answering problems and discovering essential information.

This book is our attempt to spread the word about the I-Search to you, our teacher partners and media specialist colleagues. Many of you have already asked us how we teach the I-Search process. This book will serve as a guide through the steps that we have developed in our efforts to adapt the process to the K-12 level. Through our experiences with many approaches, we offer you a repertoire of what works for us.

Many of the steps in our I-Search adaptation derive from a qualitative research study set up to investigate the results of a high-school I-Search unit. That research evidenced significant improvement in student research and writing abilities.

The study also gave us a chance to track the strategies used in teaching the unit and their effects on student approaches and perspectives about research. We noted the teaching strategies that drew positive student comment about their learning growth and also the strategies that did not seem to affect the students in their vision of research. We incorporated their suggestions on where they thought the unit could be improved, particularly in the intervention strategies when they were having difficulties and in the unit management. Students who had not experienced a significant research assignment prior to the I-Search asked for more structure. They had not learned to manage their time adequately and found themselves needing more self-discipline than they could give in ninth grade. Consequently, we have built in additional debriefing and conferencing sessions that give students a chance to assimilate what they are learning and describe their problems in researching their topics.

Inside these pages, we let students tell you what they thought about the I-Search and how they wrote about their search. It was very powerful for us to hear students tell about the positive change in their understanding and use of a research process. Through the I-Search, they gained a fresh perspective and enthusiasm for research with a confidence we have seldom seen.

The I-Search process is adaptable to research projects from early elementary through adult level classes, including graduate students. Indeed, one city in Massachusetts has institutionalized it in its schools because of its positive impact on students' research and writing improvement. Students answer their questions while building a confident personal research process and effective writing style. The first person perspective, a trademark of the I-Search, convinces many students that they are good writers by letting them use their natural voice.

PURPOSE

Making the Writing and Research Connection with the I-Search Process will guide the reader through an I-Search journey from setting the historical context of the I-Search to giving strategies and techniques to use in teaching. It also gives plans for staff development workshops when your colleagues start demanding you share your research unit successes (and they will if they are like our colleagues).

We use examples of student writing to illustrate our points and give you stories of student reactions. You will find worksheets to help your students through the essential steps to focus and guide their thinking to a higher level. You will find suggestions for ways you can adapt the process in case you plan a unit smaller than the ones we taught. We add information literacy skills and research strategies at crucial points to help students find the research success that will carry them through later curriculum-oriented research topics. This book contains our version of the I-Search and narrative from our students as researchers and writers.

SCOPE

The scope of *Making the Writing and Research Connection With the I-Search Process* covers the definition and steps of an I-Search, the connections between the writing and research processes, the presentation and assessment of student products, interventions for students having trouble, inservice training plans for sharing the I-Search with other educators, and the connection with information literacy skills.

The theme and impact of topic choice and ownership belonging to the student, not the teacher, is present throughout the text. It is the most critical factor for ensuring student success with the I-Search and the development of a successful personal research process. Having students choose topics with strong personal meaning gives students a natural motivation to solve problems and apply information to questions.

ORGANIZATION OF THIS BOOK

We present the I-Search as a major curriculum unit lasting four to six weeks with each step in chronological order. For those of you who do not have time for a full unit, you will find the individual strategies accessible for modification or abbreviation to cover student and curriculum needs. Those of you in elementary schools who want to stretch some of the strategies over several units and years will gradually build your students' skills by the upper elementary grades. Those of you in middle and high schools can plan an I-Search unit following the strategies defined in this book or add or subtract as fits your needs. To ensure a greater chance of success for students, we discuss the problems we have had so that you can learn from us about the possible pitfalls and ways to avoid and correct them.

Chapter One is a discussion of the connections and comparisons between the writing and research processes. It relates the traditional research model approach that most of us were taught in school. The chapter also briefly reports on the research process models developed and/or articulated by media specialists and media specialist educators.

Chapter Two covers the origination of the I-Search and the crucial concept of the "topic choosing you." The I-Search depends on students choosing a topic that compels them to research for an explanation or an answer. Their interest is so high that the subject area no longer belongs to the teacher, as is traditional, but is owned by the student, thus the topic "chooses" the student. This chapter also includes material on the I-Search format: what I knew about the topic originally; why I am writing about it; the story of my search; and what I learned about the topic through my search. Finally, the chapter addresses typical concerns about teaching an I-Search unit and merging the I-Search format with a research model.

Chapter Three actually starts the process with a discussion of the role of teachers and media specialist partners as facilitators and coaches for the students. The chapter presents an overview of the I-Search teaching process based on our research of Marilyn's experiences. It covers preparing students for metacognitive thinking and gives questions to help students reflect on previous research experiences for comparison purposes.

Topic choice strategies such as webbing techniques help students who do not have an immediate grasp on what they want to search. For the facilitators' benefit, writing prompts are given to help students start their thinking about their topics in their journals. Finally, the chapter includes a section on debriefing student experiences, skimming and scanning reading techniques, and conferencing techniques for the facilitators.

Chapter Four offers a number of teaching strategies and helpful worksheets for students. One of the most critical is the pre-notetaking sheet, a form which many of you have used for a variety of purposes. It helps the student focus the topic by asking in three columns what the student already knows about the topic, what the student thinks he/she does not know, and what the student wants to know. The research question develops from the "wants to know" column. This section is followed by sections on creating research questions and conferencing with students using Bloom's Taxonomy questions to challenge their critical thinking about their topics. Sections on general background reading techniques, reflective reading without notes (one of the hardest but most valuable parts of the I-Search according to students), choosing resources, and developing interviewing techniques for people resources round out the chapter.

In Chapter Five, readers learn our techniques for helping students create a plan of action for prioritizing investigation of resources, identifying the information they need from resources, and completing double-entry drafts for transfer to their learning logs (journals). A double-entry draft is a technique for discriminating among bits of information found in a resource. If the student finds something that seems to apply to her problem, she notes that information on the left side of a two-column page. In the right column, she explains why or how the information will affect her topic. This powerful tool teaches students how to put information in their own words along with their response to that information. The exercise suggestions on double-entry drafting included in this chapter raise student awareness of bias in reading material, opinionated statements, accuracy of facts and statistics, and various types of interpretations by authors.

Chapter Six contains information on assessment and evaluation of I-Search products. You will find suggestions and a discussion about final product ideas. You will see how students use the learning log to create a final paper product. You will learn about the techniques we give students for peer-editing, a higher-order skill essential for preparing their own work for final copy or presentation. Finally, there is substantial material on authentic assessment and questions for evaluating content, process, presentations, and writing.

Learning how to manage an I-Search unit makes Chapter Seven an important chapter for implementing an I-Search. It suggests unit timelines, student timelines, and the importance of debriefing with students throughout the unit to readjust schedules or help students complete their steps. Intervention techniques are included to provide a scaffolding for students and additional support. We include the collaborative planning and teaching partnership and responsibilities to be shared between the media specialist and classroom teacher. We have include the techniques for students to personalize their research process through the I-Search.

Chapter Eight covers inservice training. It gives suggestions for one-hour, two-day, and five-day workshops. It includes schedules, topics, and techniques for guiding the two-day and five-day sessions. Those of you who get hooked on the I-Search will probably be asked to share your experiences and techniques. Thus, we include these agenda and techniques from workshops we developed for our own use.

In addition to a summary, Chapter Nine connects the I-Search to information literacy. It defines information literacy and emphasizes the aspects addressed by the I-Search experience. It also connects the I-Search to other information literacy processes. For those of you wishing to strengthen your students' information literacy skills, this chapter will give you additional reasons for using the I-Search as a research/writing process for your students. As you will read, the I-Search is a very powerful tool for raising the information literacy achievements of our students.

SPREADING WINGS

We hope all of you who read this book will adopt the I-Search for your students. Give yourself patience and the willingness to improve your units each time you teach it. It will be worth it. Our experiences over the last six years have given us evidence that each time we teach it we improve. We spread our wings and our students' wings a little wider. We hope that never stops.

Each time we teach it, we are also amazed at how meaningful it becomes to our students, how much they enjoy it—even for the students who begrudge *anything* associated with school. For the first time, some of these students own their topic, their project, their content. They do this for themselves, not for their teacher. It is important to them. The process gives them a self-confidence and self-esteem associated with being the class expert on their topic. The pride is so evident in the sparkle that is in their eyes as they tell their peers about their work.

When we see the improvement in student research and writing by using the I-Search, we think it is imperative to share what we have learned with you, our colleagues. This book's strength comes from the experiences of our students that form our perspectives and the choice of techniques we use. We think that our students' experiences and our years of developing, adopting, and adapting strategies make our version of the I-Search a powerful writing/research process for elementary through high school students.

The format of the book lends itself to collaborative teamwork or individual efforts. We want you to have the tools, the strategies, and the techniques for adapting the I-Search to your needs. We want you to understand what the I-Search is and its history, what it will do for your students, what it will do for you, and the steps you need to know to teach it more effectively the first time. We want you to feel our enthusiasm so palpably that you have to try an I-Search unit so you can see its power for yourselves.

ACKNOWLEDGMENTS

This book belongs to our students and teaching colleagues who shared their progress and their reflections during our continuing learning process. We thank our students for their help and eagerness to teach us, their instructors. We give special thanks to Bettie Martin and Robert Tinkham, teachers at Stearns High School, Millinocket, Maine, and the teachers who work with us. The best reward for all of us is watching students succeed in their research quests.

1 WRITING/RESEARCH CONNECTIONS

Have you had your share of research nightmare stories to tell? Have you been looking for an antidote to the following situations?

An elementary student came to your media center to write a paper on one of the presidents. He pulled an encyclopedia from the shelf, copied a page worth of information, and gave the paper to his teacher. Later he returned to the media center to show you his grade of "A." What did you say?

A conscientious middle school student wrote a paper on recycling. The language was too sophisticated. When the student tried to write the information in her own words, she unintentionally plagiarized. What did you do?

The high school students in your English class brought a sense of individual voice to their narratives and creative papers, but when it came to research writing, their words sounded stilted. Their papers were more like exercises in cut-and-paste. How did you help them improve their writing styles and develop their critical thinking skills?

Such stories have served as the catalyst for our dialogue about the research process. What caused these research nightmares? What strategies and techniques have media specialists and teachers used to overcome the obstacles that lead to poor quality research writing?

We began our search for answers by comparing models of English and language arts curriculum guides on the one hand, with information literacy guides developed by media specialists on the other. The number of parallels between the writing and research processes defined in these guides surprised us.

COMPARISON OF THE WRITING AND RESEARCH PROCESSES

The writing process defined in the English and language arts guides and the research process outlined in information literacy guides had a number of common points. Besides the emphasis on process, both the writing and research processes stressed similar goals and objectives, employed many of the same teaching strategies, and took a similar approach to assessment. Checking *Webster's Third New International Dictionary*, we found that *process* was defined as "the action of passing through continuing development from a beginning to a contemplated end."[1] Process was the means by which English and language arts teachers and media specialists moved students from the status of beginning investigator to that of accomplished researcher, from beginning writer to author. Both processes shared similar goals and objectives.

From the guides, we noted that English and language arts teachers and media specialists wanted both the writer and the researcher to interpret, analyze, synthesize, and evaluate information on their topics. Both assisted students in moving through the processes for both writing and research by teaching them the techniques of observing, brainstorming, freewriting, webbing, outlining, charting, graphing, and notetaking. Finally, both assessed process and product during the activity as well as at the end of the experience.

In spite of the similarities, we noticed major omissions in these curriculum guides. Each rarely contained references to the other discipline's research and process models. For example, most English and language arts curriculum guides failed to reflect current research on the research process. Logical reasons existed for this omission. The process approach to teaching writing has existed for several decades, but the process approach to teaching research was reasonably new and published mainly in library literature. English and language arts teachers were not reaching into library literature for contemporary theory on the research process. The same held true for media specialists. While many information literacy skills curriculum guides mentioned the importance of the writing process, the connection between the two processes was still not clearly defined.

From our initial exploration into the relationship between writing and research, our central research question began to form. How could we use this relationship to improve the research process? Shortly after formulating this question, we found validation in a 1992 article by Eisenberg and Brown titled, "Current Themes Regarding Library and Information Skills Instruction: Research Supporting and Research Lacking."[2] Our research question above, worded a little differently, could be found in the "Research Lacking" section.

THE WRITING PROCESS

The next logical step in our investigation involved comparing the writing process developed by English and language arts teachers with various versions of the research process developed by media specialists. First came an analysis of the writing process. With the emergence and development of the *writing process approach* in the mid-seventies, language arts and English teachers had reached a consensus about the nature of that process. It consisted of prewriting, drafting, revising, editing, and publishing.

During the prewriting stage, students used a variety of strategies to select topics and generate supporting details. Some examples of prewriting techniques included, but were not limited to, brainstorming, jot-listing, freewriting, reading, notetaking, and outlining. Students at this stage articulated their ideas by sharing their plans with classmates. Conferencing with the teacher was especially important at this, and other stages, of the process. The teacher posed questions to stimulate critical thinking and help students overcome potential problems.

In the second step of the process, ideas generated through prewriting poured onto the page as students wrote a rough draft. After creating a draft, students shared their writing with each other, frequently in small groups of three or four. Their peers responded to drafts by posing questions for the writer and offering suggestions. While students shared their drafts with members of their writing groups, teachers met with individual students. During this conference, the student and teacher discussed what they liked and disliked about the draft and considered possibilities for revision.

Students used the input from peers and their teacher to begin the third stage of the process, revising. During the revision stage, students added supporting details, eliminated non-essential information, reorganized thoughts, and clarified wording. Students received input from peers and their teacher, usually on an "as needed" basis.

The fourth step, editing, occurred after one or more revisions of the composition. Students looked closely at each line of text, making more refined changes in wording and reorganizing information when it was needed. Editing also included proofreading the composition for errors in spelling, mechanics, grammar, usage, and sentence structure. Teachers seized the occasion of these errors to clarify grammatical concepts.

Publishing occurred when students shared their writing with others. Reading finished papers to the class, posting compositions on a bulletin board, and creating a class literary magazine were just a few of the many methods of publishing student writings. Sharing writing in this way brought the bonus of increasing students' self-esteem.

THE TRADITIONAL RESEARCH APPROACH

One discovery from our study of English and language arts curriculum guides surprised us. The traditional approach to the research process still dominated the current philosophy for teaching students how to write a research paper. It did not seem to include innovations from the writing process. For example, the National Council of Teachers of English still offered a traditional how-to-teach research guide, last revised in 1978. This publication summarized in linear form the traditional steps of the research process and its evolution as the steps have been taught over generations.[3]

The first step described in this publication was choosing and limiting a topic. During this step, the teacher conferenced once or twice with students, who then shared their proposed topics with classmates. Each student also created a preliminary thesis statement for her topic. During the second step, students planned for the project by surveying resources, developing a bibliography and a preliminary outline, and composing questions to guide the research. Step three included reading and notetaking. Students created a package of notecards which were graded and commented upon by the teacher. Step four included revising the preliminary outline. Again, teachers checked the outline and provided helpful comments. During step five students wrote rough drafts. Teachers scanned the drafts and commented on major weaknesses. In step six, drafts were returned to students for revision. During step seven, students typed and edited their final manuscripts. Step eight was submission of the completed paper.

This traditional approach to the research paper is still used in many classrooms and media programs.

MODELS FOR RESEARCH AS A PROCESS

From our analysis of English and language arts curriculum guides, we concluded that writing teachers have come to a consensus on what constitutes the educational writing process. In contrast, we discovered that media specialists used a variety of models for teaching the process of research. These models varied in terminology and the number of steps. Four well-accepted and one new model of the research process have emerged: Irving's *information and study skills*;[4] Stripling and Pitts' *research as a thinking process*;[5] Eisenberg and Berkowitz's *"Big Six Skills"*;[6] Kuhlthau's *information seeking process*;[7] and, now, Pappas and Tepe's *Follett Information Skills Model*.[8] Of the first four models, Eisenberg and Brown have noted: "While each author may explain the process with different terms, divide the various actions at different levels of specificity, and/or emphasize different phases of the process, all seem to agree on the overall scope and general breakdown of the process."[9] They suggested that a common process model begins to emerge. Each of the above models made a unique contribution to our understanding of the process and helped us establish the way we teach research through the *I-Search* method which will be introduced in the next chapter.

In *Study and Information Skills across the Curriculum*, Irving gave us more than a model of the research process. She helped us understand much of the philosophy behind the process approach to teaching information literacy skills. Irving stressed the link between information skills and life-long learning. According to Irving, *information skills* was "a broad term incorporating a range of subordinate or prerequisite skills; those associated with reading, writing, searching, retrieving, organizing, processing, thinking, analyzing, and presenting."[10] These skills not only contributed to students' success in school, but also to their daily lives. Thus, they were "the substance of many aspects of post-school work: further and higher education, vocational choice, home-finding, domestic problem-solving, and the pursuit of leisure and recreation."[11]

Next, she related "resource-based learning" to a philosophy of teaching that emphasized the individual learning styles of students and placed the teacher and media specialist in the role of facilitator. Instead of a teacher-centered classroom which reflected the learning style of the teacher, Irving supported a student-centered, resource-based classroom which offered "opportunities for learners to interact with resources in their own ways, and therefore more effectively."[12] Irving described a vision of the research process where teachers and media specialists helped students interact with resources according to their unique needs and learning styles.

While Irving helped us understand the philosophy behind the process approach to teaching research, Stripling and Pitts gave us the foundation for tapping into upper-level critical thinking and for implementing the research process. In *Brainstorms and Blueprints: Teaching Library Research as a Thinking Process*, Stripling and Pitts proposed a taxonomy of critical thinking skills that correlated with their research taxonomy.[13] They used this proposed taxonomy to explain student reaction to each level of the research taxonomy. For example, they said if students have researched at level one of the research scale (fact-finding), they probably will react at level one of their corresponding scale (recalling). The verbs Stripling and Pitts used to describe recalling included: "arrange, cluster, define, find, identify, label, list, locate, match, name, recall, recount, repeat, reproduce, select, sort, state."[14] For each succeeding level in their taxonomy, they listed appropriate verbs to use which gave the teacher and media specialist help in constructing activities that emphasized critical thinking by students.

The Research Taxonomy	The REACTS Taxonomy
Fact-finding	Recalling
Asking/Searching	Explaining
Examining/Organizing	Analyzing
Evaluating/Deliberating	Challenging
Integrating/Concluding	Transforming
Conceptualizing	Synthesizing[15]

From *Brainstorms and Blueprints* by Barbara K. Stripling and Judy M. Pitts. Libraries Unlimited, Englewood, CO, 1988. Used with permission.

For each step of their ten-step model of the research process, they presented a variety of strategies which teachers and media specialists could use to help students practice that step. Their emphasis on critical thinking reinforced our belief in teaching sophisticated thinking skills. Stripling and Pitts' use of the REACT taxonomy with its accompanying action verbs provided us with a process for moving students through each stage of the hierarchy.

While Stripling and Pitts supplied us with the strategies for teaching parts of the research process, Eisenberg and Berkowitz gave us strategies for using these skills in problem-solving. They used an approach called "curriculum mapping" to pinpoint the best places for teaching the stages of their research process which they called the "Big Six Skills."[16] They defined the research process as a series of steps to use in problem-solving in a variety of subject areas at all grade levels. Many media specialists have used the "Big Six" as an approach for integrating the research process across the curriculum.

Of the five models, we found Kuhlthau's "Information Search Process" to be the only model based on formal research. Kuhlthau seemed to have one of the closest links to the writing process. For example, she used Emig's study[17] of twelfth grade English students as a springboard for her research. While Emig focused on "writing from what was already known or from long-term memory,"[18] Kuhlthau stressed "composing from what we learn from information."[19]

Kuhlthau used methodologies employed by educational researchers working with process writing. She analyzed student journals containing students' reactions toward and feelings about their work. She interviewed or held conferences with students and conducted case studies tracing individual student behavior. More than isolating steps of a process, she investigated the metacognitive activities of students during the process, concentrating on feelings that evolved during research projects. Kuhlthau has been the first researcher we noticed who suggested a cross-over between the writing process and the research process through her work.

Kuhlthau's research had a number of implications for our work and posed new questions. How could we use strategies such as student journals, student interviews, and case studies to investigate the relationship between writing and research? Might student journals be more than a means of gathering data for our research? Could journals be a strategy for helping students develop their own critical thinking by reflecting on their personal research process?

It was exciting to see Pappas and Tepe's nonlinear research process model which included sections on appreciation, presearch, search, interpretation, communication, and evaluation. They designed the model in a graphical form to resemble a rainbow in an effort to underscore the nonlinear approach to gathering, using, and evaluating information. Searchers are encouraged to assess and reassess their personal information seeking process with the ultimate goal of developing their own unique style.

After studying these models, we had a pressing concern. We believed that some of them under-emphasized the important connection between the writing process and research process. We needed an appropriate model of the research process that would help us make the connection. Further investigation into the connections between the writing and research processes led to an important discovery of the writings of Donald Murray. He provided us with the critical link between the writing and research processes by defining writing in terms of information processing.

Murray's model of the writing process consisted of the interaction of four forces: collecting, connecting, writing, and reading one's writing as part of the act of revision. Murray began by stressing the link between writing and information. He said: "The primary forward motion of the writing process seems to come from man's unlimited hunger for *collecting* information."[20] People had a primal, "intellectual need to discover meaning in experience"[21] which consisted of information collected through the five senses. This led to the second component of Murray's writing process model, *connecting*. Murray continued:

> We must discriminate, select the information that is significant, build chains of information which lead to meaning, relate immediate information to previous information, project information into the future, discover from the patterns of information what new information must be sought.[22]

Writing, the third component of the process, resulted from the "primitive need to experience experience by articulating it."[23] The final component, *reading*, involved "criticism."[24] Reading their own writing forced people to reevaluate and revise their thoughts and words. Finding appropriate words to communicate their ideas contributed to the development of their *voice* or personal writing style.

Murray's analysis of writing as information processing added a new dimension to our search. Originally, we wanted to discover how the individual steps of the writing process related to the individual steps of the research process. We expected to learn how process writing techniques and strategies could be used to teach the stages of the research process. Murray showed us that we needed to move beyond our emphasis on process into how people make meaning: to understand how we make meaning of information and to trace the evolution of our thinking as we move through the stages of our writing and research. How did we make connections from the information we gathered? What role did writing play as we moved through the stages of the research process? How could writing be used to articulate the critical thinking used at each stage of our thoughts so that others could see where we have been? The writing-research process connection was much more complex than we originally had thought.

Articulation of these problems convinced us that we needed to select a model of the research process as a foundation for our own work with students. We finally chose the research process outlined in the *Information Skills Guide for Maine Educators.*[25] Based on the Washington state model, this research process has a number of important features. The model is written in terms of educational objectives and is compatible with the five widely-accepted models as noted above. The format provided a brief explanation of each of thirteen steps in clear, conversational language free of jargon associated with any specific content area. Skills were defined in terms of student objectives. Because many of the objectives paralleled those found in curriculum guides, teachers could easily identify with the material and see how it could be integrated into their own curricula. This made the material more inviting to teachers as well as to media specialists.

Our study of the process models for both writing and research provided us with background information. But now we needed to move into areas not yet explored in the literature. How would we help students understand our chosen research process model and teach them to apply their own version of it to new information problem-solving situations? We remembered Murray's words, "In teaching the process we have to look, not at what students need to know, but what they need to experience."[26] The traditional approach to the research paper was not the answer. With the suggestion of a friend, we discovered the solution to our problem in Ken Macrorie's book *The I-Search Paper.*[27] Our next chapter discusses Macrorie's I-Search and our interpretation of its use as a research process.

NOTES

1. Philip Babcock Gove, ed. *Webster's Third New International Dictionary of the English Language, Unabridged* (Springfield, MA: G. & C. Merriam, 1967), p. 1808.
2. Michael B. Eisenberg and Michael K. Brown, "Current Themes Regarding Library and Information Skills Instruction: Research Supporting and Research Lacking," *School Library Media Quarterly* 20, no. 2 (Winter 1992): 105.
3. Richard Corbin and Jonathan Corbin, *Research Papers: A Guided Writing Experience for Senior High School Students,* Rev. Ed. (New York: New York State English Council, 1978).
4. Ann Irving, *Study and Information Skills Across the Curriculum* (London: Heinemann Educational Books, 1985).
5. Barbara K. Stripling and Judy M. Pitts, *Brainstorms and Blueprints: Teaching Library Research as a Thinking Process* (Englewood, CO: Libraries Unlimited, 1988).
6. Michael B. Eisenberg and Robert E. Berkowitz, *Information Problem-Solving: The Big Six Skills Approach to Library and Information Skills Instruction* (Norwood, NJ: Ablex Publishing, 1990).
7. Carol C. Kuhlthau, *Seeking Meaning: A Process Approach to Library and Information Services* (Norwood, NJ: Ablex Publishing, 1993).
8. Marjorie L. Pappas and Ann E. Tepe, *Follett Information Skills Model Kit* (McHenry, IL: Follett Software Company, 1995).
9. Eisenberg and Brown, p. 105.
10. Irving, p. 22.
11. Ibid., p. 15.
12. Ibid., p. 18.
13. Stripling and Pitts, p. 10.
14. Ibid., p. 11.
15. Ibid.
16. Eisenberg and Berkowitz, p. 15.
17. Janet Emig. *The Composing Process of Twelfth Graders* (Urbana, IL: National Council of Teachers of English, NCTE Research Report No. 13, 1971).
18. Kuhlthau, p. xix.
19. Ibid.
20. Donald M. Murray, "Writing as Process: How Writing Finds Its Own Meaning," in *Learning by Teaching: Selected Articles on Writing and Teaching* (Portsmouth, NH: Heinemann, 1982), p. 22.
21. Ibid.

22. Ibid.
23. Ibid.
24. Ibid., p. 23.
25. Maine Educational Media Association's Ad Hoc Committee on Information Skills, *Information Skills Guide for Maine Educators* (Augusta, ME: Maine State Library, 1990).
26. Murray, p. 25.
27. Ken Macrorie, *The I-Search Paper* (Portsmouth, NH: Heinemann, 1988).

2 WHAT IS THE I-SEARCH PAPER?

ORIGIN OF THE I-SEARCH

During our first reading of the *I-Search Paper*,[1] we felt an immediate connection with its author Ken Macrorie. Macrorie's background was different from ours, but he shared our frustrations and minced no words expressing them. In the preface to his book *The I-Search Paper*, this college professor of English composition complained, "For many decades high schools and colleges have fostered the 'research paper,' which has become an exercise in badly done bibliography, often an introduction to the art of plagiarism, and a triumph of meaninglessness—for both the writer and the reader."[2] He called traditional research papers "Re-Searches, in which the job is to search again what someone has already searched."[3] Instead of wasting more time lamenting the quality of his students' research papers, Macrorie created an alternative assignment. The result was the "I-Search paper."

What was an I-Search and how was it different from traditional research? Macrorie's definition of the I-Search was simple and direct: "A person conducts a search to find out something he needs to know for his own life and writes the story of his adventure."[4] In other words, not only did the "I" refer to the story which took the form of a first person narrative, but it also referred to the personal nature of the topic. Macrorie compared his students' "need to know" to an itch that must be scratched. He called I-Search papers "original searches in which persons scratch an itch they feel, one so marvelously itchy that they begin rubbing a finger tip against it and the rubbing feels so good that they dig in with a fingernail."[5]

Macrorie eloquently articulated for us the problem with traditional research. As Irving suggested, the research process was an integral part of our daily lives. It presented itself in both simple and complicated forms. We listened to the weather report to gather the data needed to decide how to dress. We made informed decisions when buying a car by questioning salespeople, reading *Consumer Reports* and automotive magazines, and asking friends about their satisfaction with their vehicles. When faced with a serious illness, we questioned our doctors, sought out a second opinion, and read about the illness so that we could make an informed decision. What a contrast this was to the traditional research paper which, as Macrorie noted, was frequently a summary of second-hand information on topics that failed to engage our students throughout a lengthy process.

Was the I-Search the answer to our problem with format? Would it, with modifications, be our vehicle for teaching the research process, and with what age groups? It was now time to dig into Macrorie's book, to let Macrorie speak to us. Following Donald Murray's model of writing as information processing, we needed to read, collect new information, connect it with our experience and knowledge of the research process models, and write about our reactions.

A TOPIC CHOOSES YOU

Reading through the initial chapters of the *I-Search Paper*, we kept returning to one of Macrorie's chapter titles: "A Topic Choosing You."[6] To make research meaningful, a student had to have a stake in her topic. Macrorie stated, "No one can give other persons knowledge, make them think or become curious. Knowledge must reside in a person or it is not knowledge; and even if that person accumulates it, without use it is—what else could it be?—useless."[7]

What if students were allowed to write about issues and problems that truly affected their lives? We began to recall those moments in our media centers when students—and our colleagues—had an immediate need for information. Topics ranged from the mundane to life-threatening: "I need to find a way to store all my junk. Do you think your electronic magazine index would list some articles on closet organizers?" "My brother's just been diagnosed with Hodgkin's Disease. My parents are really upset. Do you have some stuff we could read?" These people devoured the materials we gave them. They wanted to share with us what they were learning and their plans for using that information. Moreover, their stories fascinated us; we wanted to know the outcomes. How could that immediacy be incorporated into an assignment?

Macrorie made a novel proposition for our students: "What should *you* choose to search? I can't say enough times that this is the wrong question. Rather ask, 'What's choosing me? What do I need to know? Not what I believe will impress others, but what keeps nagging me?'"[8] These words produced new connections. We recalled students who picked topics for the wrong reasons. "I think I'll write my paper on abortion. There's lots of books written on the topic, so I won't have problems finding information." "I'm doing the federal deficit. Mr. Adams is always harping on it. That topic will impress him." Or the worst case scenario: "My history teacher had us draw topics out of a hat for our research papers. I got 'Pete Rose and corruption in baseball.' I hate baseball!" Macrorie definitely reminded us about what was wrong with assigned research topics, even when there was plenty of room for choice within the parameters of the assignment. To be meaningful for teaching the research process, the student's topic must have arisen from a real *need* for information; information that could be used in her life.

THE I-SEARCH FORMAT

We related to Macrorie's experience with research papers: "Now I realize that other teachers and I have given so many instructions to students about the form and length of papers that we've destroyed their natural curiosity. They don't want to grab books off the shelf and taste them."[9] How many times have we heard our students groan when the teacher mentioned "research" or "term paper"? We needed an approach to research that communicated the excitement that came from hunting down information to solve a problem or make a decision, rather than merely trying to locate it. Macrorie's format of the I-Search narrative seemed to meet our need:

1. What I Knew
2. Why I'm Writing This Paper
3. The Search
4. What I Learned[10]

ADDRESSING CONCERNS ABOUT USING THE I-SEARCH

Initially, we had some concerns that high school teachers might balk at using a narrative to teach research since it was simpler to execute than other forms of expository writing. Would a narrative exercise the critical thinking skills needed for more complex forms of writing? Macrorie answered our question, "Often we talk and write our way into understanding, especially when we tell a story of human action: relating how and where it happened often shows us why, and with what significance."[11] Again, Murray's model came to mind. We believed that writing about our experiences forced us to process our thoughts. It gave us something we could return to and reflect upon. It enabled us to make new connections as we read about others' experiences. We began to recognize cause and effect and evaluate events. As Macrorie notes, the I-Search provided students with an opportunity to practice the "lifetime skills"[12] of listening, speaking, reading, and writing. Through the I-Search students learned how to conduct interviews, incorporate quotes into their narratives, and note sources.

Macrorie changed our minds about the power of the narrative. The narrative was a tool for meeting an information need, evaluating experiences related to that need, and deciding a future course of action. Developing our critical thinking skills was a natural consequence of entering into this process. The narrative also spoke to a broader audience of readers and researchers. As Macrorie noted for his students, the I-Search is more than an "intellectual task."[13] The end product was in many cases an appealing story suitable for publication in magazines and books.

The I-Search paper was more than a vehicle for teaching the research process and more than a piece written for a teacher or shared with fellow students in writing groups. The I-Search was a viable format suitable for publication. Macrorie had definitely extended the boundaries of our work.

MERGING THE I-SEARCH FORMAT WITH A RESEARCH MODEL

Macrorie presented a convincing argument. We decided to use the I-Search with our students. But before we implemented an I-Search unit, we chose to merge Macrorie's format with the stages of the thirteen-step research process outlined in the Maine model. Would the Maine model of the research process fit with the I-Search paper's format or would we need to make modifications in the format? Keeping these questions in mind, we returned to Macrorie's text.

We easily matched the stages of the presearch phase of the research process with the first two stages of the I-Search paper.

I-Search Format	*Steps in the Presearch Process*
What I Know	1. Formulation of the Central Research Question
	2. Relation of the Question to Prior Knowledge (includes consulting broad resources such as general encyclopedias)
	3. Identification of Key Words and

Why I'm Writing
the Paper

Names (includes skimming and scanning resources)
4. Integration of Concepts (includes creating outlines, webbing diagrams, lists and/or other organizational strategies)
5. Development of Questions to Organize the Search
6. (When Needed) Re-exploration of General Resources

But was it a perfect match? Based on our personal experiences teaching research, we knew that much of the success or failure of a research project hinged on the successful completion of the *presearch* stage of the research process. At this stage, students selected a topic, found a focus, wrote questions to guide their research, and created a tentative organizational pattern. Without these components, students lacked direction and purpose, and became overwhelmed by a sea of information. The end result in such cases was frustration accompanied by the failure to complete the project or the creation of a paper consisting of numerous quotes strung together—the "cut-and-paste" approach to research.

The successful completion of the six steps of the presearch process was the first step toward a quality end product. But what happened when Macrorie's two steps were added, and students selected a personally meaningful topic? Our thoughts returned to Murray's model of information processing consisting of collecting, connecting, writing, and reading, and Kuhlthau's model combining thoughts, actions, and feelings. Merging Kuhlthau, Murray, and the Maine model with the I-Search format, gave us the following plan of action:

- Students keep a written record of their thoughts, actions, and feelings (Kuhlthau's model) as they move through the stages of a combination of Macrorie's format with the stages of the presearch process.
- As they collect information by consulting general encyclopedias and skimming and scanning resources, students write about what they know and do not know about their topic.
- As they begin to comprehend their motivation for researching their subject, students write about their information need.

- Students reread what they have written, share it with fellow students, their teacher, and the media specialist. Finally, they make revisions in their central research question and additional questions to guide their research.

To our delight, the pieces fit. Murray's and Kuhlthau's combined theories merged with Macrorie's vehicle for teaching the research process. But would we be able to integrate these components into the remaining stages of the process?

Returning to Macrorie, we studied his approach to "*The Search*" phase of the I-Search. Macrorie stressed the interview as a primary means of information gathering, in addition to the use of libraries. Furthermore, he advocated using dialogue from interviews in the I-Search paper's text. While this was an interesting approach to writing the I-Search, we found his approach too restrictive. Our students needed a wider variety of sources and strategies. They needed to develop a wide range of information literacy skills omitted from Macrorie's explanation. We wanted our students to use writing as a means to foster critical thinking and trace their thoughts.

We turned to the Maine model to guide us in merging information literacy skills within the remaining phases of the I-Search. When we merged the remainder of the Maine model with the I-Search format, the following relationships appeared:

I-Search Format	**Steps in the Research Process**
The Search	*Search*
	7. Locate Resources of Information
	8. Search for Relevant Information
	Interpretation
	9. Select and Evaluate Information (checking for currency, point of view, bias, author's/producer's motives)
	10. Interpret, Infer, Analyze and Paraphrase (identifying main ideas, supporting details and opinions; relating content to the research questions)
	Application
	11. Organize Information for Applications (synthesizing information

from sources, organizing it, and using an effective method of presentation)

What I Learned

12. Apply Information for Intended Purpose (making a clear, well-supported presentation; drawing conclusions based on information; evaluating the project and search process; being able to apply content and process to new learning situations)

13. Appreciation (recognizing the relationship between the research process and life-long learning; valuing information)

We wanted our students' I-Search papers to contain more than the answers to their research questions. We wanted them to write about how they selected, evaluated, and used their information. Drawing upon Murray's model, we wanted them to reveal how their thinking evolved as they read, collected, connected, and wrote to evaluate their thinking. Following Kuhlthau's model, we wanted them to communicate their thoughts and feelings as they acted upon each step of the research process. We wanted our students to value information and feel confident in their abilities to use information to solve problems and make decisions throughout their lives. Our gut reaction said the I-Search was the vehicle to use, but we still needed strategies for implementing it. Macrorie's college composition class strategies did not transfer completely to K-12 students' needs.

It was time for us, the authors, to move beyond Macrorie's methods and tap into our own experiences, one of us as a former high school English teacher turned media specialist, and the other as a former media specialist turned college professor. Both of us taught the I-Search as a research process each year to our students. We were continuing to build our teaching methodologies, and wanted to offer the following chapters as guidance for you in building your own repertoire. We knew media specialists from the elementary level to the senior high level who used the I-Search effectively and productively for teaching research.

It took time to develop expertise and good teaching relationships with classroom teachers in implementing this process. Some used it as a foundation for more traditional research assignments. Others used it as an investigatory process for younger students.

Our research studies show the I-Search to be quite successful in giving students a strong sense of effective research strategies. Defining the word *'research'* might still be difficult for them but they have a sense of what works and why it works. They use that sense to develop their research sophistication as they continue in school. And that is what it is all about.

NOTES

1. Ken Macrorie, *The I-Search Paper* (Portsmouth, N.H.: Heinemann, 1988).
2. Ibid., preface, no page.
3. Ibid., p. 14.
4. Ibid., preface, no page.
5. Ibid., p. 14.
6. Ibid., p. 66.
7. Ibid., p. 14.
8. Ibid., p. 71.
9. Ibid., p. 55.
10. Ibid., p. 64.
11. Ibid., p. 99.
12. Ibid., p. 71.
13. Ibid., p. 77.

3 STARTING THE PROCESS

We believe that the I-Search method is a natural tool for collaboration among media specialists and teachers as well as a means for teaching research and writing. When teachers and media specialists work together, they share responsibilities for planning, teaching, and facilitating throughout the unit. A collaboration between an English teacher and a media specialist gives students two teachers for the I-Search unit, two facilitators, two "idea" people, more individualized attention, and, consequently, a more complete process. Collaboration ensures that the I-Search unit contains both writing and research process goals. Students see this team as teachers with a vested interest in their success and respond accordingly.

From our experiences described in the previous chapter and a qualitative study of students in Bettie Martin's English classes in Millinocket, Maine, we identify the key stages in the I-Search process and develop the strategies and techniques to facilitate its implementation. We hope these steps will serve as a model for teachers and media specialists who want to develop their own I-Search units in a collaborative spirit.

The steps we present are not so much a "formula for success" but a method of getting you started in creating your own set of teaching strategies. They are the result of our four years of experience in teaching the I-Search. We constantly modify and add to the strategies we use because the essence of being a process person is to evaluate and make the changes required to design a successful unit. We invite you to build upon our strategies to create a process that will meet the unique needs of your students.

Each unit you teach probably will require different strategies depending on content and information literacy objectives. Some of you will find that the I-Search lends itself to subject-area investigations quite productively and gives the students more opportunity to claim ownership of their research. Others of you will want to concentrate on using the I-Search to develop a research foundation. As you will see, topic choice plays a very critical role in building a solid set of personal research strategies.

RELATIONSHIPS AMONG THE PARTICIPANTS

The relationship between students and teachers is vital to the I-Search process. We view the teacher and media specialist as facilitators. Our students are collaborative partners in developing the process because we need their input. Students tell us when they are frustrated or confused, and we draw upon our experience to guide them through obstacles. Facilitation means that we constantly work with our students to assess their progress. To meet the needs of our students, we modify our plans, activities, and objectives when necessary. The I-Search cannot thrive in a rigid curriculum that restricts change and experimentation.

Communication is a part of facilitation. By asking questions of the students, we guide and engage them in thinking about what they are doing and how they are doing it. Asking questions keeps the ownership of the project with the student, not with the teacher. Facilitation means helping students discover their own course of action, not telling students what is wrong.

PREPARING FOR THE UNIT

We identify activities that work for a majority of our students. Nevertheless, the activities are not ends in themselves. They are strategies for facilitating the process as we experience it. If a strategy or technique does not meet the needs of an individual student or group of students, we assist students in finding alternatives. By listening to students, we know how to adjust our teaching to meet their needs.

To grow as educators, we must question our assumptions about our students, what we are teaching, and what our students need. Some of the best process teachers also take this route. Atwell says, "I paved the way [for change] through writing and reading about writing . . . through uncovering and questioning my assumptions, through observing kids and trying to make sense of my observations, through dumb mistakes, uncertain experiments, and underneath it all, the desire to do my best by my kids."[1] She gives herself permission to experiment with new methodologies. We give ourselves permission to experiment and make our students collaborators. We give them an investment in making the process a success. Moreover, we are better role models: Our students perceive us as problem solvers specifically because we include them in the problem solving.

As a tool to help you develop your I-Search strategies and assess your progress, we encourage you to keep a learning log during the course of your I-Search units. Observing students and recording observations helps educators discover techniques that work and techniques that need improvement. Recording comments from conferences also serves as an effective method for monitoring students' progress. Moreover, rereading the log entries frequently helps you and your partner make new discoveries about strategies and connections that will strengthen the unit. Sharing your learning logs with students helps students feel a part of the process. This involvement and interaction among students, the media specialist, and classroom teacher is a critical component of the I-Search unit. Interaction in the form of conferencing will be discussed in more depth later in the chapter.

OVERVIEW OF THE I-SEARCH PROCESS

In the spring of 1994, we conducted an in-depth, qualitative research study of Martin's students. Based on the data from the study, we drew a diagram of the I-Search process and its key components as they took place. This diagram has evolved as we continue to teach the I-Search. It reflects how we now feel about the key components of the process and gives you a visual overview.

Our study isolates four key sections of the process: choosing a topic, finding information, using information, and presenting the I-Search product (in the Maine experience a written paper and oral presentation). This process results in effective transference of the research process to other situations requiring information problem solving. Each key section has a number of strategies for facilitating that stage of the process. Some of the strategies recur throughout the I-Search. A typical example is the practice of reflective reading. When students do general background reading, it helps for them to decide on a focus for research questions. Indepth reading helps them search out specific information to answer the questions.

The remainder of this chapter stresses these four main subdivisions and their associated strategies.

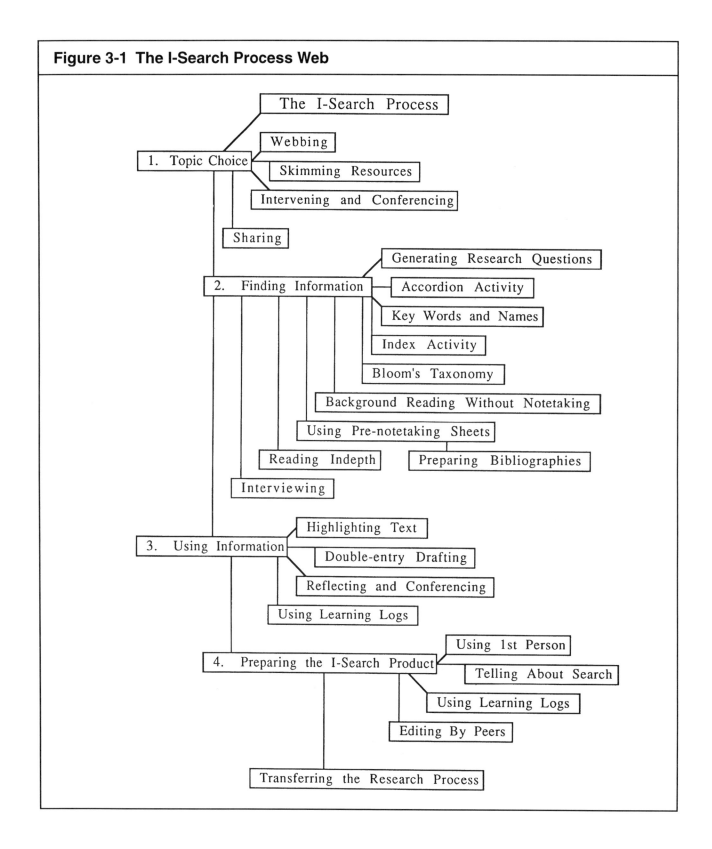

Figure 3-1 The I-Search Process Web

PREPARING STUDENTS FOR METACOGNITIVE THINKING

The I-Search is different from many classroom assignments because it requires the students to think about their thinking. To introduce our students to the concept of metacognition, we ask each student to keep a log in which they record their actions, thoughts, and feelings as they move through the I-Search unit. The log provides access to their thoughts as they react to the information they collect and attempt to apply it to their problem. It also serves as a record of their search strategies, both those that are successful and those needing modification. When they put together their final product, they refer to the log for much of their narrative. Depending on the requirements for the unit, the final version or product might even be an edited version of the log.

REFLECTING ON PREVIOUS RESEARCH EXPERIENCES

We like to have students reflect on their research experiences for a first activity in our I-Search units. This reflection sets the stage for a more productive appreciation of the new research methodology. To get students thinking reflectively and critically about research strategies, we have students comment about research assignments they have completed in the past. We ask them to respond in their learning logs to the following prompts:

1. What are some of the research projects you have done?
2. From these projects, what does *research* mean to you?
3. Describe one of your research successes. Why was the experience positive?
4. Describe one of your research failures. Why was the experience negative?

The responses from Martin's ninth grade classes revealed a frustration with traditional research methods. Very few students valued their previous research projects. They recalled little content and could not relate the work to their lives. They could not adequately describe a good research process:

> Research, I believe, is when you [get] an assignment that you have to use an encyclopedia or dictionary.

> [Research is] to look in books and find the perfect information to copy.

> Research is no big deal. It's not very tough to do. All you have to do is look [up] your subject in an encyclopedia and then write your information in your own words. I think research is easy and boring.

If left alone, these attitudes would influence acceptance of the I-Search methodology. To help students make the transition to the I-Search, we explain how the I-Search is different from many of their past research assignments. Unlike assignments that require them to collect and summarize information, the I-Search requires them to use information to solve problems and make decisions. This approach to introducing the I-Search helps us establish the idea of information problem solving early in the unit. We frequently find that we need to reinforce the problem-solving aspect in contrast to the preconception of research as the reporting of facts.

Sharing research successes and nightmares from students' personal experiences also helps us explain many of the objectives for the unit. For example, our students' comments on topic selection frequently reflect the importance of picking personally meaningful topics. One student noted: "A positive research assignment that stands out in my mind was an autobiography that I did last year. It gave me a chance to find out about my past and relatives. . . . I found out things about myself that I never knew before." Another student enjoyed his science fair project on the behavior of fish because it made him a better fisherman. A third student found his math project on Pascal's triangle "long and boring" until he was able to relate his information to what he was learning in a computer programming class. Such responses are a natural introduction to "the topic choosing you."

Research nightmares are also a tool for previewing the obstacles students encounter during the process. "I couldn't come up with a topic." "I didn't know how to start." "It was hard to put [the information] in my own words." "My science teacher made us collect leaves and identify them. We all had to scramble down to the library before all three of the books on leaves were taken out." "I always wait until the night before to do it. Then my parents get mad because I stay up all night." "I had lots of stuff on notecards. But I couldn't figure out how to organize them!"

We use student comments to preview some of the challenges our students will face as well as to reinforce the purpose of the learning log and our approach to assessment. We explain that all researchers encounter obstacles. The goal is to find strategies and techniques for overcoming them. Then we explain that the learning log is an excellent place for discussing their problems and describing possible solutions. Students can also evaluate the actions they take to solve the problems.

We give them credit for keeping a log of their activities, making sure they include their failures as well as successes. The enticement of credit usually encourages hesitant students to try the strategy. Most students are impressed that their media specialist and teacher care about their thoughts and feelings. They also like the idea that we will provide them with individual assistance throughout the project. Sharing their thoughts and the promise of individual assistance establish a positive atmosphere for the unit.

CHOOSING A TOPIC

Choosing a topic "that itches" might be simple for adults who bring many life experiences to an I-Search and face many problems both big and small in their daily lives. But what about the students who come to us with fewer life experiences and little practice in acknowledging them? Some students draw a blank.

Our first attempt at using brainstorming techniques and browsing through current magazines and newspaper articles for ideas failed to produce meaningful topics for our students: while students were successful in finding subjects, they chose "hot topics" such as the Bermuda Triangle, serial killers, and rock groups instead of subjects related to their life experiences. The I-Search calls for a different approach to topic selection. To avoid this pitfall, we now use the following webbing activity to aid many students in topic selection.

WEBBING ACTIVITY

We have students create an experience web in their learning logs consisting of several major milestones in their lives. These milestones can be associated with an experience, an event, a person, a significant item, or a place.

These are the instructions we gave each student:

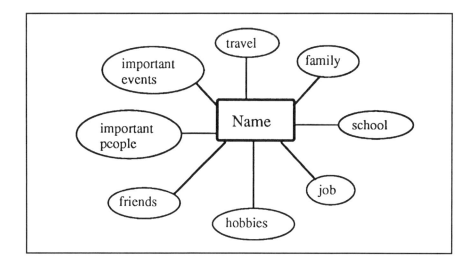

For each major balloon on the web, list a milestone in your life. Leave space around each of these milestone balloons so that you will be able to surround each of them with other, connecting balloons.

1. Around each milestone, make balloons listing the first two or three connections that pop into your head, such as people, places, or incidents related to the milestone.
2. Around that first layer of connected balloons, create a second layer for each balloon consisting of experiences concerning the milestone.
3. Fill a third layer of balloons around each balloon in the second layer with how the milestone is significant. How did it affect you? What did it show about your strengths or weaknesses, plans for the future, career choices, and/or personal goals?

We explain the activity by modeling the web. Sometimes we ask another faculty member to be the subject of our web. Our students enjoy watching an adult go through the process. It is also a good way of introducing a teacher, administrator, or guidance counselor to the procedure. We ask questions of the person being interviewed and record the responses on a web drawn on the blackboard or an overhead transparency. Our goal is to obtain as many details about the chosen milestones as possible.

By modeling questioning strategies, we prepare students to use questions to help each other make their webs. We stress that the key to the development of a good web is the use of questioning skills. The following is an actual dialogue:

Questioner:	What is an important event in your life?
Subject:	I won the moose lottery! The odds were a thousand to one that year.
Questioner:	Tell me about the lottery.
Subject:	Each spring Maine has a lottery to draw the names of people who can go on a moose hunt in the fall. Everyone was excited when I won the lottery. But when I finally went on the hunt and saw a moose, I couldn't kill it. I just stood there and whispered, 'Look at the moose.'
Questioner:	Why do you think you couldn't shoot the moose?
Subject:	The moose was so dumb. It just stood there on this dirt road staring at us. I just couldn't kill it.

Below are the responses as they appeared on the web:

The questioner looks for opportunities to find relationships between items on the web. Students observing the interview ask questions of the participant. What items on the web arouse their curiosity and require more information from the participant? What information do they want to know about the participant herself? This activity helps them think about the webs they will draw and how they will help each other develop the webs in greater detail. For example, does the participant think about her encounter with the moose in terms of her personal values? Does she know why she cannot shoot the moose?

After generating as many responses as possible to each balloon on the web, our entire group looks for repeated ideas or themes that can lead to an I-Search. This participant tells about her love of animals. She describes her fondness for cats and enjoyment of wild animals. A possible I-Search topic related to animal rights emerges. What are this individual's expectations for society's food needs in relation to animal rights? This question becomes her central research question.

Modeling this webbing diagram takes about forty minutes. To follow up on the activity, we have students work on their own experience webs. We do this in class so that students can work with friends and ask each other questions. Meanwhile, we circulate about the room facilitating the activity. We help students generate details by asking them questions about their activities and assist them in recognizing "themes" that appear on their webs. At the end of the period, we give students the assignment of taking their web home and sharing it with their parents/guardians, a close friend or relative, or a favorite teacher.

Involving other adults in the process, especially those close to the students, is particularly helpful. Frequently students fail to recognize the important events and people in their own lives. In spite of his web, one student thought about searching one of those "hot topics" such as UFOs, reincarnation, or signs of the zodiac, until he spoke to his parents: "They really didn't like any of my topics but gave me two topics they were curious about. First my father told me that he was curious about Ireland because his ancestors came from Ireland. . . . Next I talked to my mother. She told me that she had been curious about my cousin Kristy who has autism. I liked this topic quite a bit because I was curious about why she acts the way she does." He decided to explore the autism topic with the added bonus of guaranteed parental interest in the final result.

We give students plenty of time to reflect on their choice of topic. Many students need time outside of school to think about what they should do. Sometimes this reflective period results in a powerful choice. Sara recounted her experience picking a topic in her learning log:

> I was walking through the house looking at old pictures when I saw a picture of my Gramma Shirley (my Dad's mother). I asked my mom what she died of, and that's how I came up with ALS (Amyotrophic Lateral Sclerosis). From that point on, I was curious about what the disease does to you, how it develops, the first symptoms, and whether or not it's hereditary. The idea of ALS being hereditary played a huge role in my decision of this topic. I was really scared about whether I was going to die in my late forties. Why be scared!? Another major factor was I wanted to find out about the disease that killed my grandmother. Whether she suffered and what she went through. I don't think I will ever stop searching for facts until they find a cure and know what causes it.

This reflection time is an important factor in Martin's lesson planning. She begins her I-Search unit the week before Thanksgiving vacation. The webbing exercise is timed so that students can complete the assignment by discussing their web with an important adult over the vacation. They can speak with relatives, many of whom are gathering for Thanksgiving dinner, and ask them about family events and their opinions of those events.

After students complete the webbing assignment and isolate two or three possible topics, they need to "process" what they have done by recording their actions, thoughts, and feelings in their learning logs. We give them writing prompts to help them record how they chose their topic. What we want them to think about is how they selected their topics and why they prioritized them in the way that they did. Why did they choose the topic in one major balloon over another? We also want them to think about how valuable the strategies were that they used to find their topic.

We keep flexible with these steps. Some students will come back from their holiday with an entirely different topic as a result of conversations. Other students find a topic of immediate importance in their lives and do not have to go through a decision-making step. In these cases, we have the student concentrate on the specific topic and try to find layers of relationships within the topic. This helps the student settle on research questions through the pre-notetaking strategy that follows.

WRITING PROMPTS

We use the following "sentence starters" to help our students reflect on their progress in choosing a topic. We have students expand the sentence starters into a paragraph with their thoughts and opinions on the strategies.

1. I learned the following information about myself through my web:
2. I think webbing helped/did not help me find a topic because:
3. I want to consider the following two or three topics for my I-Search:
4. My first choice of a topic is _____ because:
5. I know the following about my first choice:

We recommend giving students time to write in class with the media specialist and teacher present to facilitate the process. At this stage facilitation includes:

- working with individual students to draw out subjects that should be included in the learning log;
- asking questions to help students generate details;
- having students with good learning log entries read their responses to the class, thus providing others with good models.

DEBRIEFING

The end of the writing period is a good time for debriefing. For us, debriefing involves a time for students to share their thoughts on the process with us and their peers. Where are they in the process of topic choice? What strategies are working for them—e.g., the web? What problems are they encountering and how can they overcome them? What is their next step? If a student says that she is frustrated with a lack of information in the web, is the student talking with peers, parents, favorite teachers, or you to gather suggestions? By discussing their successes as well as their frustrations or confusions, we identify problems and work as a group to solve them. The debriefing time also establishes an atmosphere of collaboration among the media specialist, teacher, and students.

SKIMMING AND SCANNING RESOURCES

Students are now ready to use media center resources for the initial exploration of their topics in order of preference. For students whose topics have chosen them, scanning material about their subjects in general encyclopedias and specialized reference materials, browsing abstracts and articles on electronic magazine indexes, and skimming relevant chapters of books start what might be called a "feeding frenzy." The more they learn, the more they will want to know.

This initial investigation of potential sources is also our opportunity to insert the missing information skills. We direct students to appropriate print and nonprint information resources. We observe students to determine those who will need help finding the right topic. Students who move too quickly from topic to topic or who find all three of their initial choices uninteresting will need individual conferencing.

CONFERENCING

Recognizing the need for individual conferencing and knowing when to intervene are key components of the process approach to teaching research. Kuhlthau interprets intervention as "mediation into areas where individuals cannot proceed on their own, or can advance only with great difficulty."[2] Conferencing with individual students, debriefing students at the beginning or end of a class, and reading learning logs are strategies which help us determine when and with whom to intervene.

The initial exploration of potential topics usually involves two days of working in the media center with time for students to share their topics with the class and explain how the "topics chose them." Students sit in a circle and each shares his or her topic with the entire class. If time is limited, we divide the class into groups of four or five and have students share their topics with their group. Allowing students to interact with their peers at this phase of the I-Search process serves several purposes. Finding the words to communicate their topics and goals to peers forces students to articulate their thoughts. Input from classmates, usually in the form of questions, can help students clarify vague language, identify a related idea worth exploring, and hear about a good source of information. A positive response from peers validates a student's work and choice, thus increasing her level of comfort.

In the next section, we discuss more of the presearch process. We include the use of a pre-notetaking sheet, resource searching, and background reading.

NOTES

1. Nancie Atwell, *In the Middle* (Portsmouth, NH: Heinemann, 1987), p. 4.
2. Carol Collier Kuhlthau, *Seeking Meaning: A Process Approach to Library and Information Services* (Norwood, NJ: Ablex, 1993), p. 155.

4 NARROWING THE TOPIC

After choosing a topic, we move our students to the second phase of the research process, which consists of narrowing the topic and finding a focus. To emphasize the importance of this phase, we use as an example our own frustrations as students. Our teachers would move us into thesis statements and tentative outlines before we knew how to narrow our research focus and we could not do it. We realize now that the cause of our failure was not our lack of ability; we did not have enough information on our topics. The presearch stage was missing.

The Maine model of the research process, which we adopted, breaks presearch into five components: (1) Formulate a tentative central research question; (2) Relate the question to prior knowledge; (3) Identify key words and names; (4) Integrate concepts; and (5) Develop questions to organize the search. Then we add our own sixth step: (6) If necessary, make adjustments to the central research question and its focus.

The steps in this stage, however, are usually not sequential. Finding a focus is an evolutionary process that reflects Murray's model of writing as information processing. As students collect information, they connect it to prior knowledge, much as constructivists advocate. After they write about their initial impressions, they read more about their topic. New information can lead to a new discovery or conflict with previous assumptions, forcing re-evaluation. Thus, as students learn more about their subjects, they revise their research questions and refine their focus.

PRE-NOTETAKING SHEET

Early in our research, we discovered an effective strategy for finding a focus in Rankin's article on critical thinking.[1] We also found other models in the literature that were very similar, e.g., the *What I Know* sheet from Call.[2] We incorporated Rankin's strong research activity into the I-Search process and called it pre-notetaking. Rankin and her teaching partner had their middle school students list what they knew about their subjects and then added what they did not know. Our students tended to generate more questions for the *Don't Know* column than they could answer through an I-Search. Thus, we set up a third column for them to choose four or five related questions they wanted to focus on in their research. At this stage of the process, students also developed a working bibliography. The back of the pre-notetaking sheet provided a space for students to list their sources.

Name:		**Pre-notetaking Sheet**
Topic:		
What I Know	What I Don't Know	What I Want to Answer in My Research

---

Sources: Record all print and nonprint materials used during the pre-search stage. Place a check next to the items which best answer your research questions.

_____ 1.

_____ 2.

_____ 3.

_____ 4.

_____ 5.

_____ 6.

_____ 7.

_____ 8.

_____ 9.

_____ 10.

Approved by: _____

From a student in a graduate course, we learned about another valuable strategy to help students create questions related to their topics. Each student writes her topics at the top of a sheet of paper. The papers are passed around the room so that other students can each add a question about the topic. With a large class, students work by rows or within their writing groups. After each student writes a question under the topic, she folds the paper in an accordion shape with only the topic showing. This prevents the next student from borrowing another student's question. Although there might be some duplication, students end up with additional questions for exploration about their topics. They select appropriate questions from their "accordions" and add them to their pre-notetaking sheets.

After completing the accordion activity, students still need to create more questions for the _Don't Know_ column of their pre-notetaking sheets. They frequently pose the question, "How can

I write questions when I don't know that much about my topic?" This is the perfect opportunity to introduce students to the use of electronic and print indexes to discover key words and names associated with their topics. Using overhead transparencies and copies of sample tables of contents and index pages, we demonstrate how to use key terms to create potential research questions for a sample topic. We also include a segment on how to find key words and names by skimming and scanning magazine articles.

Building upon the previous lesson, we model how to develop questions for the pre-notetaking sheet using another sample topic. We ask students to locate key words from an index or table of contents duplicated on handouts and distributed to the class, or reproduced on an overhead transparency. Next we have them combine each key word with one or more of the question starters *who, what, when, where, why,* and *how* to create their own questions. We record their questions on a pre-notetaking sheet drawn on the blackboard. To help students go beyond creating questions with *who, what, when, where, why,* and *how,* we have them think in terms of comparing and contrasting, tracing a change over a period of time, predicting, and classifying. After generating as many questions as possible for the *What I Don't Know* column, we ask students to find four or five related questions that could serve as a focus for research on this topic and have them provide a justification for that focus. We also show how to move beyond questions that ask only for facts to questions that require analysis, synthesis, and evaluation. Following is a handout summarizing how to create research questions, which we give to our students.

Melissa's story illustrated the fascinating evolution of a student's thinking as she developed her pre-notetaking sheet. Melissa wanted to explore a topic related to young people with disabilities. She wrote on her pre-notetaking sheet:

> My friend _____ has Down's syndrome. I know it doesn't mean he lacks certain abilities. _____ has shown me that he is very active and able to do many things you wouldn't expect him to do. Some people with Down's syndrome are very capable, like Chris Burke, the TV actor in *Life Goes On.*

Working with InfoTrac, the electronic magazine index, Melissa created potential research questions from the following key words and phrases: "causes," "care and treatment," "diagnosis," "genetics," "complications," and "risk factors." Her *What I Don't Know* list contains these and other questions: "What are the

How to Write Research Questions

1. Use key words and names found in indexes to create questions to guide your research. Combine these words with *who?, what?, when?, where?, why?,* and *how?*

   Below is a partial listing of key words found under "cystic fibrosis" in the TOM version of InfoTrac:

   CYSTIC FIBROSIS
   - bibliographies
   - care and treatment
   - case studies
   - cases
   - diagnosis
   - genetics

   SAMPLE QUESTIONS based on key words from index:
   1. How do doctors treat cystic fibrosis?
   2. What is the genetic background of the disease?
   3. What is the cause? When is it first diagnosed?
   4. How do doctors diagnose cystic fibrosis?
   5. What happens to people with cystic fibrosis? What can be learned from case studies?
   6. What bibliographies are available on the subject?

2. Survey newspaper and magazine articles and create questions from headlines, items in bold type or italics, information in the introductory paragraph, illustrations, charts, graphs, photographs, and the concluding paragraph.

New York Times, Wednesday, January 6, 1993:

NEW FOSSILS POINT TO EARLY DINOSAUR

Remains of Dog-Sized Reptile to Shed Light on Ancestor of Giant Creatures

by Warren E. Leary

Washington, Jan. 6—Scientists said today that they discovered the 225 million-year-old remains of the world's most primitive dinosaur, a dog-sized creature that they said would shed new light on the dinosaur's early family tree.

SAMPLE QUESTIONS:
1. What do new fossils tell scientists?
2. How large were the fossils?
3. Who made the discovery?
4. When and where was the discovery made?
5. Why are these findings important?
6. How old are the fossils?

Name: Melissa		**Pre-notetaking Sheet**
Topic: Down's Syndrome		
What I Know	**What I Don't Know**	**What I Want to Answer in my Research**
1. One of my friends, ___ has Down's. I know it doesn't mean he lacks certain abilities. 2. ___ has shown me that he is very active and able to do many things you wouldn't expect him to do. 3. Some people with Down's are very capable, like Chris Burke, the TV actor in "Life Goes On." 4. Human chromosome 21 has something to do with this disorder. It has to do with genetics.	1. What are the causes? 2. When do you find out a child has Down's? How do doctors diagnose it? 3. How do doctors care and treat people with this syndrome? 4. What role does genetics play in this syndrome? 5. What are some of the complications and risk factors? 6. How does having Down's affect your personality? 7. Can students with Down's take classes with "normal" students? What is "normal"? 8. To what extent can people with Down's live normal lives? Work? Live alone? Have children? Raise a family? 9. Do people with Down's get embarrassed by it? 10. How do people react to those with Down's? How do people with Down's react to others?	1. Can people with Down's syndrome live "normal" lives—live alone, work, marry, have children? 2. Should children with this disorder be in the same classroom with "normal" children? What is "normal"? 3. How does having Down's syndrome affect your personality? 4. How are people with Down's treated by other people?

causes? When do you find out a child has Down's syndrome? How do doctors diagnose it? How do doctors care for and treat these children? What role does genetics play? What are some of the complications and risk factors?" Through individual conferencing with her media specialist and teacher and sharing her thoughts with peers, she discovered the questions she wanted to answer through her research. "Can people with Down's syndrome live 'normal' lives? What is 'normal'? Should children with this genetic disorder be in the same classroom with 'normal' students?" Her focus evolves from questions that can be answered with a few facts to questions about complex issues requiring in-depth analysis.

CONFERENCING DURING THE PRE-NOTETAKING STAGE USING BLOOM'S TAXONOMY

Conferencing with each student is essential after completing initial drafts of the pre-notetaking sheets. During our interventions at this stage, we help our students create questions that will challenge their critical thinking. Our assessment tool is Bloom's Taxonomy of Educational Objectives.[3] Most of our assessment is based in the cognitive domain, which consists of six increasingly complex categories: *knowledge, comprehension, application, analysis, synthesis,* and *evaluation.* The chart below provides a summary of the taxonomy as presented in a companion guide to the *Information Skills Guide for Maine Educators.*[4] The upper half of the chart defines the six levels of critical thinking from the simplest to the more complex skills. The lower half suggests a list of words used to generate questions or create activities for each step on the hierarchy.

An assessment of Melissa's work on Down's syndrome reveals the complexity and sophistication of her thinking. The earlier questions on her pre-notetaking sheet represent thinking at the lower level of the taxonomy: *knowledge* and *comprehension.* Later questions, however, reflect the upper range of the taxonomy. Asking what is 'normal' requires the *analysis* of various definitions of normalcy. To create her own, unique definition of the term, she must *synthesize* concepts. "Should children with this disorder be in the same classroom with 'normal' children?" reveals

Bloom's Taxonomy Chart					
Knowledge of	**Comprehension**	**Application of**	**Analysis**	**Synthesis**	**Evaluation**

Terms
Facts
Methods
Procedures
Concepts
Principles
	Use
	  implications
	Verbal to
	  math
	Chart/graph
	Justify
	  concept
		Theory to
		  practice
		Law to
		  situation
		Problem
		  solving
		Doing chart/
		  graph
		Demo-ing
		  method
			Recognize
			  assumptions
			Recognize
			  poor logic
			Distinguish
			  fact
			Distinguish
			  inference
			Evaluate
			  relevancy
			Analyze
			  structure
				Write theme
				Present
				  speech
				Plan
				  experiment
				Integrate info
					Consistency
					Data support
					Using
					  standards
					Setting criteria

Remember
Recall
Define
Describe
Identify
Label
Match
Name
Outline
Reproduce
Select
Underline
List
	Grasp
	  meaning
	Explain
	Summarize
	Interpret
	Predict
	Paraphrase
	Translate
	Transpose
	  format
	Retell
	Project
	Account for
		Use in new
		  situation
		Try
		Perform
		Develop
		Manipulate
			Break into
			  parts
			Re-organize
			Identify parts
			Analyze
			  relationships
			Recognize
			  patterns
			Examine
			Simplify
			Discern
			Compare
			Check
			Uncover
			Determine
			Assess
				Create a new
				  whole
				Present
				  uniquely
				Propose a
				  plan
				Establish
				Combine
				Produce
				Re-organize
				Formulate
					Judge with
					  purpose
					Decide
					Prioritize
					Classify
					Arbitrate
					Accept/reject
					Diagnose

thinking at the *evaluation* stage. Her pre-notetaking sheet shows she is capable of reaching the most complex stage of cognitive thinking.

When we conferenced with Melissa, we indicated where her questions fell on the taxonomy and explained the significance of that placement. Her awareness of the taxonomy as a tool for creating questions that challenged her to think helped her transfer her question-asking ability to other activities. Being aware of the depth of the research she wanted to undertake gave her confidence. She was proud of her ability to think critically.

Because Melissa's pre-notetaking sheet needed no revision, the conference ended with a question "What is your next step?" She shared her plans. Books were helping her answer some of her questions, but she also wanted to interview _____ and members of his family. We suggested she interview the special education teacher in her school who worked with two Down's syndrome students. She agreed that this was another good source of information and enthusiastically began her work. Melissa developed excellent questions for her pre-notetaking sheet with little assistance from her media specialist or teacher.

But what about students who encounter problems? We believe much of the success or failure of any research process depends on the quality of presearch preparation and prior knowledge of the topic. In spite of the I-Search format, students whose background knowledge is inadequate or whose focuses fail to involve problem solving or decision making will still produce "cut and paste" products. Conferencing with these students takes the form of an intervention. The goal is to help them expand their knowledge enough to create questions that promote critical thinking.

GENERAL BACKGROUND READING

We used the strategy of background reading to give students an opportunity to read generally without notetaking to build basic knowledge in their topic areas. Students who did not have an adequate prior knowledge of their topic had greater difficulty filling out the *What I Want to Know* column on the pre-notetaking sheet. For example, the student who wanted to investigate her grandmother's disease had very limited knowledge but a strong personal interest. General reading helped her fill in the information gaps and construct her research questions. It also helped her discover the depth of her topic and whether she should make changes in its scope. She learned the basic vocabulary and found a direction to take in the focused reading that followed. Another student claimed she needed to change her topic because she did not understand what she was reading. Our conference revealed she merely needed an introduction to the specialized vocabulary associated with her topic. A third student claimed he could not read the material he found on his topic. We discovered he was trying to read his most difficult article first instead of beginning with those with a more general perspective.

READING WITHOUT NOTETAKING

We provided several class periods for students to read, but we told them not to take notes, a habit some students found hard to break. We did, however, give them time to reflect on what they had read by writing in their learning logs at the end of each class period. Students in the study thought this was the hardest thing they had had to do during the I-Search, but reported that it helped them think and learn how to express themselves. Here, students began to value their opinions and analyze and synthesize the information they were reading. Reading without stopping to take notes personalized the information they found and gave them a platform to test out the information against their feelings and prior knowledge.

At the end of each reading period, we asked students to address the following questions in their learning logs: What new discoveries did they make? How did they react to what they read? How could they use that information to help them solve their problems? What other pieces of information did they remember and how could they apply them? What other questions emerged as a result of new information? Writing reactions to the material formed the basis of student ownership of information and led to problem solving. Finally, we had them note the best sources they had explored that day.

Reading without notetaking is a vital strategy for getting students to think about information. This strategy increases students' ability to respond personally to the topic. By easing the burden of sorting through many isolated pieces of information, students also gain a frame of reference for dealing with information sources. They learn the common viewpoints associated with their subjects. They find points of comparison and contrast.

CONFERENCING TO HELP WITH QUESTION FORMATION

We have worked with a number of high school freshmen who complete I-Searches related to careers. They frequently have problems developing challenging research questions because their initial questions are usually factual in nature: What is the salary for this career? What skills do I need? Are there job openings in this field? What are the working conditions? What kind of education do I need?

Mike's story shows how conferencing moved a student from a consideration of factual information into the application of information to solve problems and make decisions. The conference began with Mike explaining the contents of his pre-notetaking sheet: "I selected my topic 'cause my father gave me books on welding and diving, and I really want to dive and weld. . . . I really want to be an underwater welder." This student already knew some information about his favored job.

For the *What I Don't Know* column, Mike created factual questions using information from general encyclopedias and the *Occupational Outlook Handbook* published by the U.S. Department of Labor. He was particularly interested in learning about the skills needed for this job and the kind of education he needed to compete with other underwater welders. Because many of his questions could be answered with just a few facts, we posed a question to stimulate Mike's critical thinking. "How will you use your information to plan your career?" Mike thought he could compare the skills he already had with those needed by underwater welders. He could find his strengths and weaknesses and work to improve skills that are weak. We asked him, "What is the first step in initiating this plan?" After some thought, Mike decided he should talk to his guidance counselor.

To help Mike remember the decisions he made during the conference, we had him create new research questions which we recorded in the *What I Want to Answer Through My Research* column. He developed the following questions: "What are my strengths and weaknesses? What can I do to improve my skills? How can my guidance counselor help me?" To conclude the conference, we praised Mike for his progress.

Reinforcement was an important element of the process, especially for a student like Mike who was classified as "low ability" in this particular school's tracking system. As a follow-up to the conference, Mike's English teacher asked him to review with her the decisions made during the initial conference. He enjoyed sharing his pre-notetaking sheet with her because he was proud of its contents. The teacher was able to make an addition to the sheet by suggesting that Mike interview the welding instructor at the vocational school which is housed at the high school. She offered to take Mike to the vocational area and introduce him to that teacher.

Mike was one of the earlier participants in our I-Search units. Since his conference, we have modified the pre-notetaking procedure. We now conclude each conference by using a copy of the Bloom's Taxonomy Chart to point out placement on the critical thinking hierarchy. With this change, we would have ended Mike's conference by explaining how he has progressed from creating questions reflecting *knowledge* and *comprehension* to questions reflecting *synthesis* (developing a plan of action) and *evaluation* (of his strengths and weaknesses). With the addition of this strategy, Mike would eventually gain a sense of the hierarchy of critical thinking and could become a self-assessor of his critical thinking progress.

We also remind students that the pre-notetaking sheet can be revised and modified all through the process. For many, the focus will evolve as new information is gathered. They will want to add new or revised questions to the *What I Don't Know* and the *What I Want to Answer* columns.

REFLECTION ON THE PRE-NOTETAKING PROCESS

After drafting and revising the pre-notetaking sheet and conferencing with the media specialist and/or teacher, students need time to reflect on the process. We ask students to respond to the following writing prompts in their learning logs:

1. Describe how the pre-notetaking sheet helped you find both a focus for your topic and research questions to investigate.
2. Summarize what happened during your conference. What problems or obstacles did you identify during your conference? What strategies will you use to overcome them?
3. Evaluate your experience using the pre-notetaking sheet and your experience conferencing with your media spe-

cialist and/or teacher. How were these techniques useful? What suggestions would you make to improve these steps?

4. Now, what are you going to do next?

We have students read their responses to the class or share them with the members of their writing groups. Listeners are invited to respond through class discussion or by writing brief responses in other students' learning logs. Then, we conduct a debriefing session posing the question: What conclusions can we draw about pre-notetaking and conferencing based on our reflections?

Our objective in debriefing is to identify obstacles that are still causing problems for students at this stage. Debriefing is a type of formative evaluation or ongoing assessment of the process and is critically important to the student and to the teaching team in analyzing the strategies used in the process. We find that some students need extra time while others are ready to move on. We modify our timeline to keep the class together and facilitate future instruction at the point of need for all students. This stage of the process is the place for a class break from the I-Search. Spending one or two days reading a short story or one-act play or writing poetry provides a break from the intensity of the I-Search unit. It allows students who are somewhat behind to catch up before we give them the next major strategy.

FOCUSING ON RESOURCES

After finding a suitable focus and developing challenging research questions, students need time to focus on their resources. As a result, we include time for reading, viewing videos, listening to audiocassettes, and experiencing multimedia computer programs. Students collect materials and apply information to their research questions. They experience an intense period of discovery, and the excitement of finding information relevant to their questions. At this point, students bond with their topics.

The media center is the best place to work during this period. The students' hunger for resources is considerable. Thus, we create an atmosphere that is informal, yet controlled, to encourage students to share their discoveries. We help with resource suggestions and ask students to talk about what they are doing.

At the end of each class session devoted to the investigation of resources, we ask students to reflect on the progress they have made in their learning logs. What new discoveries did they make? How are these discoveries influencing their thinking? What new connections are they making as a result of collecting new information? Do they need to modify their action plans in light of new information?

Having students periodically return to their learning logs and read past entries is a crucial part of the process. Short-term memory is fleeting. By having students review their logs, we ensure that their insights will be etched in their long-term memory. If they need a reminder, the insight will be in their learning log. Reflection is, in our opinion, one of the most powerful strategies we emphasize through the I-Search because it leads to critical thinking.

MAKING INFORMATION ACCESSIBLE

When students find critical resources, we facilitate the students' ability to take the information with them by photocopying appropriate articles from magazines in our hard-copy collection or printing out essential sections from CD-ROM sources. The students' experience with the pre-notetaking sheet and conferencing prevents most indiscriminate copying. Students have the focus for their research that we find missing in many other projects. We watch for and intervene with the few students who appear to photocopy mindlessly. In most cases, these students are still having problems articulating their focus.

INTERVIEWING AS AN ALTERNATIVE RESOURCE

The focusing period is a good time to seek out human resources and to schedule interviews. It is also a good time to schedule a lesson on interviewing techniques to calm students' hesitancies for the interviewing process. Some students know who they want to interview and other students need suggestions of appropriate people. Our student interested in Down's syndrome knew people who were "experts" on her topic. The underwater welder received suggestions from us. Other students learned about human resources through their friends or through local and state databases.

Much of the planning for interviews takes place during the conferences or in a class session. We review the following stages of the interview process and discuss answers to the corresponding questions:

1. Preparing for the interview—how do you plan to make the appointment (e.g., by telephone, in person, or through an introduction performed by a third person)? What information should you know about the person being inter-

viewed? What do you plan to accomplish during the interview? What questions do you plan to ask?

2. Conducting the interview—what are the rules of etiquette for an interview (e.g., introductions, body language, listening skills, and thanking the interviewee)? How will you record information (e.g., taking notes or recording the conversation on audiocassette or videotape)? How do you obtain permission to tape an interview?

3. Following the interview—should you send a thank-you note? If questions evolve as a result of new information, is a follow-up interview by phone or in person possible?

Technology is changing the methods students use to conduct interviews. One freshman at Stearns High School wanted to interview someone 300 miles away; unable to travel, the student conducted the interview via facsimile. Increased Internet access facilitates e-mail interviews. Telephone interviews are another alternative. With permission, an inexpensive microphone that fits between the ear and the telephone receiver is a good tool to tape telephone interviews.

Some shy students feel uncomfortable conducting person-to-person interviews. E-mail and fax interviews are good alternatives for these students. When the technology is not available, we try to match them up with someone they know, such as a teacher, neighbor, or relative who might be an "expert" on their subject.

Interviews can produce interesting results. Our student studying Down's syndrome videotaped her interview of the Down's student and his family. We helped her dub a copy of her videocassette so that she could share it with others. As a result of this interview and personal interactions with people having Down's syndrome, she became an advocate for individuals with disabilities. Our student investigating underwater welding impressed the vocational instructor with his enthusiasm and knowledge. As a result, the instructor created a special program just for him. Mike started his vocational training as a second semester freshman instead of waiting until his junior year, the traditional time for students to join the vocational program. For these students, the I-Search was only a beginning.

In our next chapter we enter the search stage and begin by addressing the creation of a plan of action.

NOTES

1. Virginia Rankin, "One Route to Critical Thinking," *School Library Journal* 34, no. 5 (January 1988): 29.
2. Patricia E. Call, "SQ3R + What I Know Sheet = One Strong Strategy," *Journal of Reading* 35, no. 1: 50–52.
3. *Taxonomy of Educational Objectives; The Classification of Educational Goals* (New York: D. McCay, 1974).
4. Maine Educational Media Association, Committee on Information Skills, *A Maine Sampler of Information Skills Activities for Maine Student Book Award Nominees, 1992–1993. Part 1.* (Augusta, ME: Maine State Library, 1993), p. 28.

5 USING INFORMATION

Notecards! So necessary, yet so difficult to teach! Some of our students would ask, "What do I do with all these notecards?" or they would exclaim, "Gee, haven't I done a good job! Look at how many notecards I've collected," expecting the highest form of praise from us. But when we received their papers, we were stunned with their lack of insight and interpretation. We also found a disturbing amount of cutting-and-pasting. We asked ourselves, did they plagiarize intentionally or were we to blame? Had we given students the tools to assimilate their information? This section includes our strategies for correcting this ever present problem.

CREATING A PLAN OF ACTION

Students begin the next stage of the research process, *using information*, by creating a plan of action. We ask students to prioritize their resources in a manner that meets their information needs. If they are dealing with complicated subjects, they can arrange their resources in order of general to specific or in order of simplest in organization and writing style to more sophisticated in content and structure. If they are dealing with controversial material or theories, they can group together authors with comparable ideas or opposing viewpoints. Their plan of action makes their use of information more efficient.

Placing the plan of action in their learning logs assures students constant access to remind them of the path they decided to follow in using their resources. Anytime they want to modify that plan, they note it in their learning log.

USING PHOTOCOPIES AND HIGHLIGHTING TEXT

Do you remember having to take notes on cards for term papers? Many teachers still require students to use notecards as a strategy for choosing important pieces of information from a variety of sources, synthesizing the information, and organizing it into an original paper. Some students thrive on this method, but for others, information taken out of context loses its meaning. They fail to see the connection between the isolated bits and pieces.

We suggest teaching students who cannot handle notecards how to highlight text and add marginal notes. Students take the photocopied materials they have gathered during their presearch and then highlight important facts: potential answers to their research questions, phrases, or sentences that produce a strong positive or negative reaction; and comparable and contradictory information found in other resources. The marginal notes provide a reminder of the reason for highlighting the text: "author agrees/disagrees with [another author]," "that's disgusting!" "excellent idea," "I predict," "need more information on this," and other responses.

Our students summarize and comment in their learning logs on what they highlight. To ensure that our students remember the source, we have them include bibliographic information with their reflections; e.g., "First I read 'Mandatory Seat Belts in Jeopardy' by John Hale in the May 4, 1995, edition of the *Bangor Daily News*. I learned . . . " Students summarize the information that answers their research questions in a lively narrative, and the problems with plagiarism seem to disappear. However, we sometimes need to intervene with students who have tendencies to highlight everything. We remind them to concentrate on material that answers their research questions.

DOUBLE-ENTRY DRAFT

We want our students to go beyond merely answering their research questions. We want them to evaluate their sources for such things as currency, accuracy, point of view, bias, and the difference between fact and opinion. We also want them to discover how they feel when they connect new information to their personal experience and knowledge base. How does their thinking evolve as they move through Murray's process of collecting, connecting, writing, and reading? How is this information helping them to solve the problems or make the decisions related to the topic that chooses them, to reach the proverbial itch that needs to be scratched? To solve our problem, we turn to a technique developed by English teachers: the double-entry draft.

The double-entry draft is a vehicle for helping students make meaning out of text. While most activities associated with the I-Search are taught through short lessons, double-entry drafting needs time for thorough training. It is a skill developed through practice, and needs monitoring to keep students progressing. When they first begin, their responses are very brief. They need practice in adding details to their responses. They need help in moving their comments into the upper levels of Bloom's Taxonomy. To assist you in designing your lesson for teaching the double-entry draft, we include an example of a training session as it occurred at Brewer High School in Maine.

DAY 1

Step 1: We demonstrate how to prepare the double-entry draft, and explain how to use it.
Directions: Divide a paper in half lengthwise. Label the first column *Content* and the second column *Response*.

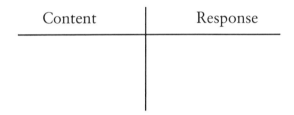

In the *Content* column, students record a word, phrase, or one or two sentences that provoke a positive or negative reaction in them. In the second column, they explain the reaction. On the first day, each student focuses on making sense out of what she reads by relating it to her personal experiences or personal knowledge of the text's subject. Possible responses include, but are not limited to, the following:

- A main idea and why it's important
- A paraphrase of a complex passage, e.g., one with difficult vocabulary or sentence structure
- A possible explanation of a confusing passage
- A personal experience that gives meaning to a section of the text
- A comment on the author's writing style and why the student likes/dislikes it
- A prediction that can be made based on evidence from the text
- A reaction to a passage that produced a strong emotion (anger, frustration, joy, comfort) or reaction (agreement, disagreement)
- A question generated as a result of their reading

Step 2: We model the process described in step one.

This is one example of what happened at Brewer High School when we modeled the process. In the spring of 1995, a class of freshmen English students experienced double-entry drafting using an article from the local newspaper on mandatory seat belts. After reading the headline but not the text, students briefly discussed what they knew about the seat belt law in Maine. Teenagers up to the age of eighteen were required to wear seat belts, but adults did not have to wear them. The legislature wanted to make seat belts mandatory for adults, too.

As students listened to the article being read aloud, they used a pencil or pen to place a check mark on their copy next to any parts of the text producing a reaction. Working as a group, they wrote several examples of content and responses on a double-entry draft drawn on the blackboard. One boy volunteered an emotional response to the first sentence in the article which announced that the House could not decide on having a mandatory seat belt law. "Figures," he said. "Politicians can never decide anything." Other students agreed that politicians seemed to spend most of their time debating and not enough time making decisions.

The article reported that the House bill was in "limbo." "What docs 'limbo' mean?" asked a student. After speculating on the meaning using context clues and confirming the definition using a dictionary, the students moved to another passage. Another boy reacted strongly to a "primary enforcement" clause in one seat belt bill which would allow a police officer to stop any vehicle with a passenger without a seat belt. "Dumb. Waste of time!" Others agreed that police had more important things to do "like arrest criminals." "You wouldn't say that if you had been in an accident. A seat belt saved my life," countered one of the girls. This statement resulted in several students sharing their personal experiences involving automobile accidents. Because students were obviously making meaning of the text, we gave them time to create their own double-entry drafts.

After approximately ten minutes, we asked them to share the results of their individual drafts. Over half of the class reacted to the strong statistics within the article. The following sentence appeared in the content column: "Maine has the lowest estimated seat-belt [sic] use in the country, at about 35 percent, compared with a 66 percent national average."[1] Responses ranged from surprise to condemnation of people who did not wear seat belts as well as condemnation of the government. "I didn't know that. I thought at least more people wore their seat belts than that." "This sounds right. I never use my seat-belt [sic]. None of my family or friends do either." "That is bad because that means that 65 percent of those people, if they got in an accident, would be hurt worse." "If engineers would design a crash proof system with the government, there wouldn't be a problem. But it's the government's fault." "Who cares? It's your choice to wear it, not theirs."

The responses resulted in several minutes of lively debate on the pros and cons of seat belt use. As we approached the end of the period, we had enough time for one final response to a portion of the text. A number of students reacted to a member of the House who suggested the wearing of helmets inside automobiles. "Come on, get real. Like people would do that?" said a student who took the comment literally. Another student volunteered an alternative interpretation, "This is funny. Is it crazy, or an exaggeration to get the point across?" Students finally agreed that the Representative was using exaggeration to make a point; however, there was still a disagreement over whether this sarcasm was a good persuasive tactic.

As the period reached its conclusion, five minutes remained for debriefing. Did students find the activity useful? Students agreed that they enjoyed this approach to discussion. We were pleased that *every* student had something to share with the class. The shy, quiet students as well as those who always seemed to respond to a new activity with the comment "This is dumb!" made constructive contributions. They interacted with the text, derived personal meanings, and shared them with the class. Some changed their opinions based on new input from the discussion. The class was a success. The debate experience led to increased critical thinking.

DAY 2

Step 3: We give them strategies for evaluating information.

We were successful in helping students use double-entry drafts to derive personal meaning from the text. The next step was to give them a strategy for evaluating that information. For the follow-up lesson we gave them a second article from *USA Today* on the use of seat belts.[2] This time we gave them a list of possible questions to answer in the response column and asked them to focus on evaluating the article.

- Is the information current?
- What is the author's purpose, e.g., informative or persuasive?
- What is the author's point of view?
- Is the author biased?
- Does the information in the article agree or disagree with other sources? Give examples.

- Is the author and/or publisher reliable? What is his or her reputation?
- How do the graphics (pictures, charts, graphs, photos) contribute to an understanding of the information?
- Is the author's presentation logical? Explain.
- Does the author support her generalizations with facts and examples? Justify your response.

After answering students' queries regarding the questions above, we had students work independently reading the article and creating double-entry drafts. Then they placed their desks in a circle, and we shared the results. The responses proved that students in this group tended to be visual learners; almost all commented on the chart and graphs accompanying the article. They found the chart titled "Seat Belt Use in the USA," which presented the results of a 1992 survey by the National Highway Traffic Safety Administration, an efficient method of comparing the use of seat belts in various states. However, several noticed that the statistics were dated; therefore, they thought they might not present an accurate picture of present use.

Others questioned the accuracy of the statistics: the National Highway Traffic Safety Administration's survey indicated that 70 percent of "motor vehicle drivers and front-seat [sic] passengers wore belts in North Carolina" while that state's officials thought the figure should be closer to 65 percent. Based on this discussion, one student wondered how the officials in North Carolina gathered their information. Did the officials include passengers in the back seat? Several students compared information on the chart with figures in the previous day's article which were different for the state of Maine. Perhaps the figures from the local newspaper's article were more current or the data were gathered and analyzed differently. Because the local newspaper failed to give a source for this figure, it was difficult to analyze. The statistics "can't be rechecked," noted one girl on her double-entry draft. Another student noted that North Carolina must have a primary enforcement law because police set up 2,000 checkpoints to catch people not wearing belts. A third student wondered if checkpoints meant the same thing as roadblocks.

DAY 3:

This lively debate created a situation where students were using thinking skills to analyze, synthesize, question, and evaluate. At this point, we gave them three newspaper articles on helmet laws: The first was an editorial, the second was a straight news report, and the third was an analytical piece using factual information. When we had students analyze the articles, they praised the inclusion of opposing points of view in the analytical piece because it gave balance. But the students transferred this concept to the factual piece describing an event and wanted opposing points of view included where doing so would not have been appropriate. Thus, they mistakenly felt the factual report was biased. They did not recognize when the author had a responsibility to report an event and did not need to include a balanced perspective. Out of the three articles, they had the most trouble with the editorial which was opinion. They confused opinion with facts. We had to work with them on how to recognize the difference between the two.

With the help of double-entry drafts, they discovered they could form their own interpretations of the material they read. Those interpretations had value and led them to further discoveries about the information they gathered. They no longer trusted material as fact without questioning its authority and source. Equipping students with these tools was essential to their ability to form their own perspectives on their I-Search problems. It facilitated products that did not concentrate on cut-and-pasted information.

Finally, we had students practice and apply what they had learned in class in the following homework assignment:

FOLLOW-UP ASSIGNMENT ON DOUBLE-ENTRY DRAFTING

1. Select an article you have highlighted. Because you have already prioritized your resources, you will probably want to begin with the first source on your priority list.
2. Complete a double-entry draft from your choice.
   a. Include one or two personal reactions to the information.
   b. Include at least one related to the evaluation of the information.
3. Write an entry in your learning log using the information from the double-entry draft.
4. Include comments about how the double-entry draft helps you understand what you are reading.
5. Submit your learning log entry to your media specialist or teacher for comments on your progress.

We monitored the early double-entry drafts, especially the first draft done independently, to assess students' critical thinking skills. We wrote our reactions to the student responses in the form of questions designed to challenge their thinking. For example, we followed a brief, undeveloped response with a request for more details. We also analyzed responses using Bloom's Taxonomy. Responses located on the *knowledge* and *comprehension* levels of the taxonomy were followed by our questions at higher levels. Then we asked them to elaborate on their original responses. We were constantly pushing students into the next level of critical thinking by asking questions.

EVOLUTION

Josh's story showed the evolution of thinking as he moved from his research questions to the double-entry draft to the learning log entry. Josh was a precocious young student interested in extra-sensory (ESP) perception. At first we tried to convince him to select a more personal topic, but he persuaded us that this was a valid subject for a student with a strong interest in science. Before our first conferences with him, his research questions were at the *knowledge* and *comprehension* levels: "What are some of the tests for ESP? Are there different tests for different types of ESP?" Afterwards, Josh revised his questions: "What is the difference between science and pseudo-science? Do scientists have an accurate way of measuring ESP? Does ESP really exist? Is it a valid scientific phenomenon?" These questions reflected analysis and evaluation. He would have to develop criteria for judging a scientific phenomenon.

Below is an early entry from Josh's learning log:

> I then read *ESP* by Michael Arvey, a short book from the *Great Mysteries Series*, c. 1989. I learned about Dr. J. B. Rhine of Duke University. He [is] one of the first to initiate serious attempts to study ESP. One experiment he devised was the use of cards. These cards, Zener cards, are blank on one side and have one of five symbols printed on the other. Either a cross, a circle, a star, a square, or wavy lines. Rhine's test was quite easy. Each ESP candidate would be asked to "guess" the symbol on randomly selected cards, without seeing it. . . . I was very surprised to read about one of Rhine's subjects, Adam Linzmeyer, who correctly answered 119 out of 300. The odds of doing that are about 75,000 to 1. Another of Rhine's tests involved PK or psychokinesis. Psychokinesis defined is the ability to move matter by just one's mind. Rhine tested to see if people could willfully influence the way dice fell when rolled. This book also talked about how Rhine's work has been really criti-

cized by critics. Some criticism came from his subjects being able to see through the Zener cards. Also, Rhine's fascinating outcomes have never been duplicated by other researchers.

We did not criticize Josh's original content, nor were we concerned about writing or spelling errors. We wrote the following response in the margin of his learning log: "Good beginning! You are finding answers to your research questions. As for the criticism of Rhine's work, this brings out an important point. Is there criteria for scientific validity? How can one judge whether or not a scientist has devised an experiment that produces accurate results? Perhaps one of the science teachers can help you answer these questions." This response marked the beginning of a written dialogue between us as Josh addressed our suggestions. We stressed articulating ideas and concepts. We withheld our attention to writing errors until the draft of the final I-Search paper.

Electronic mail accounts will improve the use of conferencing as a check for student progress and a vehicle for communication to assist students with their journey. When all the students in a class have an account, the teaching team can open an I-Search class dialogue using e-mail, create work groups for support, and make themselves more individually available for student help. We would estimate that the value of conferencing during the I-Search project would double with the class time constraints eliminated.

TRANSITION FROM DOUBLE-ENTRY TO LEARNING LOG

The transition from the double-entry draft to the learning log entry is a simple process. Students take home their double-entry drafts with the ideas from conferencing or our marginal notes, reflect on the information, and add their choice of content to their learning log. They write at least one entry for each source. Then they ask us to read and assess their new material. Sometimes they read entries to the class or share their entries with their writing groups. As students grow more proficient at writing double-entry drafts and the accompanying learning log entries, they work more independently. The important element is reflection time; you do not want them to write both the learning log entry and double-entry draft at the same time. They need time to process their ideas and reactions.

At the same time, there has to be a climate of acceptance in the classroom for this strategy to succeed. If a student receives ridicule, teasing, or unfortunate giggles from peers, sharing fails and students close their minds to the I-Search. Topic choice is even more important to prevent this. If all students have a vested interest in their topics, they will want their peers to respect what they experience and to support their sharing. That desire prevents spoiling someone else's sharing time.

We find that learning logs are as unique as their subjects and the personalities of their authors. One of our students had a particular information need. Susie was born with a streak of white hair which stood out from her brown tresses. She thought some ancestors had possessed a similar trait. Was the streak hereditary? Would her hair turn white at an early age like her mother's? From the *Encyclopaedia Britannica* she discovered that her streak was a phenomenon called Piebald trait. But she had problems understanding the genetic explanation that followed. After a conference with us, Susie explored the media center's materials on Mendel's Laws and the vocabulary of genetics—i.e., dominant and recessive traits. The corresponding learning log entry from one particular book chapter was revealing: "The chapter took a lot of time to understand and for me to be able to write it in my own words, but now I understand it fully. . . . When I did other, earlier research in the *Encyclopaedia Britannica,* they related my white streak to being caused by a single dominant gene, now I understand more fully what that means."

Susie was ready for a more sophisticated explanation of Mendel's Laws. After working with two other resources, she moved from comprehension to application by creating a diagram of her family's genetic history as it related to hair color. Susie calculated that she had a 50 percent chance of inheriting white hair at an early age. Not satisfied with complete reliance on media center sources or her own interpretation, she told us that she would check her work with one of the biology teachers who specialized in genetics and heredity. Perhaps he could help her answer her remaining questions.

During conferencing, we indicated to Susie that she had used her learning log as a vehicle for disentangling some complicated background material on genetics. She had identified key words to use when seeking out further information. She was able to apply her new knowledge to her family's genetic history. And Susie would continue the search because of a discovered reference to Waardenburg's syndrome: Parents with a white forelock of hair may produce children with hearing problems. This information could affect her future plans.

Nicole, who is adopted, posed the following research question: How are different people affected by adoption? As a ninth grader, Nicole had reached a level of maturity that made her curious about a number of personal issues related to her adoption. With the help and support of her parents, she began by examining the adoption records they had kept.

> I dug out all of my adoption records and looked through them, along with my brother's adoption records. It was strange. I haven't looked at that stuff for so long—most of it I hadn't even seen before. There were letters from the adoption agency notifying my parents of their acceptance, telling them that it still may be a long wait before they received a child. I saw all that I know of my past and my birth parents—two pages of brief and general information. It was kind of emotional, really. I began to think and wonder about this woman who gave life to me. What does she look like? What is she doing? Does she still think and wonder about me? I may never know the answers to these questions, but they will always be in the back of my mind. I began to realize what my adoptive parents had to go through and how painful it must have been waiting, never knowing when they would get their child.

In spite of her openness, Nicole struggled with feelings she could not articulate until she read a book on the subject. She wrote:

> I really liked this book because the author described the feelings of being adopted perfectly. One thing he talked about was the uncertainties of which words to use when talking about adoption. . . . If I say my father was 6'2", it sounds like he's dead or something. If I say my father is 6'2", it sounds strange because I can't picture him—all that I know about what he looks like has come from paper, words that were written fourteen years ago. . . . These are just examples of little things that can be confusing.

The remainder of Nicole's investigation into resources helped her articulate and understand other complex emotions related to adoption. She interviewed two teachers, one of whom was adopted and had recently been united with her lost sisters and brothers, and one who had adopted a child. She read about people who felt abandoned by their birth parents. She read about adoptive parents who kept information about birth parents from their adopted children. After relating this material to her personal experience, her respect for her adoptive parents increased:

> In all of the reading and gathering of information I've done about adoption, I've learned more and become more aware of everyone's feelings who is involved with adoption. My own feelings have become clearer. I know that I'm very lucky and I wouldn't have chosen any other parents even if I could have, and wherever my biological mother may be, I know that she had to love me greatly to give the sacrifice that she did. I feel very fortunate that my parents have always been very honest with me about my adoption, and I have always looked at it as a good thing which has happened to me.

Nicole concluded with some predictions about her future:

> When I began my research, I felt that I wanted to know more about my biological parents, but now that need has somewhat subsided. Reading about different adoptive situations and realizing that most adoptees feel that need to know more about where they came from has helped me come to terms with myself. I have read about different ways of going about finding this information, but now I feel content with who I am. At this point I don't think that I will ever do any searching for information or digging into the past, but then again you never know!

Nicole's I-Search was more than a project for learning about the research process. It helped her analyze and articulate her feelings and evaluate her relationships with both her adoptive parents and the biological parents she had never met. For now, her "itch" had subsided, but she had developed the skills needed to continue the search if this "itch" struck again.

These stories lead us to the important final stage of the I-Search process: the written paper, which not only gives students one last opportunity to review and evaluate their work, but evolves into a finished product suitable for publication and/or presentation. In the next chapter, we give you our suggestions on final products and how they can translate to lower grade levels.

NOTES

1. John Hale, "Mandatory Seat Belts in Jeopardy," *Bangor Daily News*, Thursday, May 4, 1995, sec. A1, p. 3.
2. Lori Sharn, "N.C. Buckles Down on the Law," *USA Today*, October 22, 1993, sec. A, p. 3.

6 PRESENTATION AND ASSESSMENT OF PROCESS AND PRODUCT

THE FINAL PRODUCT

Although the traditional product envisioned by Macrorie is the I-Search paper, the I-Search lends itself to final products in a variety of formats. All types of products give teachers the opportunity to stress information literacy skills that transfer to more traditional assignments. Computer presentation packages and oral presentations, as well as written products, provide excellent opportunities for students to apply their information in a clear, well-supported way. No matter what the final product, the I-Search process promotes use of thinking skills. When we plan an I-Search unit, we explore all venues to find the presentation format that fits the assignment's purpose and ability level of the student.

With the written product, the I-Search presents a unique opportunity to have students discover their natural abilities to express themselves in writing. Writing in the first person gives a student a chance to write about his feelings and tell a story from his own perspective. For the first time, students who have writer's block discover the fun of telling their audience what they have found and how it relates to them. When we concentrate on process, our students know they can improve and revise their content as meanings change for them. The lack of factual recitation prevents the stiff unnaturalness of traditional term paper writing. We receive strong satisfaction from watching students respond to other students' appreciation of what they have to say and how they say it. Their confidence and new self-esteem floods through the process.

USING THE LEARNING LOG TO CREATE A FINAL PAPER

With our ninth graders, we choose to have the final paper be an edited version of the learning log. The learning log contains students' thoughts, reflections, and notes from their reading. It is their record of their search strategies including their degree of success. In it, they have recorded their initial webs and their research questions. They have written paragraphs on why they wanted to research their subject and what they wanted to discover. The learning log is a document representing their experiences, containing the story of their journey, what they have found, and their feelings about their topics. It is a realistic tool to help students move from notes to a more formal paper.

To help them edit their learning logs, we have students create a sequential web or an outline of the contents, whichever strategy is more comfortable for them. The linear learners gravitate towards the outline and the visual learners use the web. This helps them organize their material and find places to fit the major pieces. The resulting product is a step-by-step evolution of how they solved their problem. It is the story of their search.

At the heart the I-Search, as intended by Macrorie, is the first person narrative. First person narration gives the author a chance to express thoughts and feelings from a personal viewpoint. It encourages natural language. Writing flows more smoothly and easily. Authors do not have to worry about the stiffness of third person perspective when they try to convey their interpretations and applications of information to problem solving. Audiences read with more interest and involvement.

Unfortunately, by ninth grade many students have already been acclimated to the necessity of eliminating the "I" perspective in research writing. For those students who have been taught that "I think" and "I feel" are taboo, it is very difficult to approach a paper that requires them to value their own perspective and write in the first person. These are generally the students who claim that they cannot write. They fight the idea of having to do a paper before they discover their opinions count with the I-Search.

Topic choice is critical with these students. Helping them value their ideas on a subject is immensely easier if they have true ownership of their topics. They crave the information to solve a problem. An academic topic or a "hot" topic is not as critical for them as finding out how a grandmother's illness destroyed her life or how adoption might be explored. When they truly "own" their topics, they apply the information they find to make sense of their own lives. That happens naturally through reflection in their learning logs. Transfer to a final product becomes much easier. Topic ownership is the primary factor when it comes to students feeling at ease with first-person writing.

Some students have difficulty maintaining the first person point of view in their I-Search writing. They may start off using the first person, then revert back to a traditional third person report; or they may use the third-person report style all the way through their paper. These perspective problems also appear in their learning logs. We use the logs to spot these problems and provide intervention before it becomes serious, especially with students who have experience writing papers that report facts without forming those facts into new ideas.

We suggest using questioning strategies to assist students who have problems writing in the first person. We ask them: "How do you feel about this material?" "How does this information apply to you?" "What do you think the author means by this statement or passage?" "What ideas have you had about this topic?" These are the same questions we ask in the learning log when we spot a student having trouble relating the information to a problem. We give them time to revise without penalty.

PEER EDITING

Macrorie stresses peer editing as a strong technique to foster writing quality in the final product. Using peer editing gives us an additional opportunity to help students write in the first person. Their classmates sometimes can guide them in the use of this point of view better than their teachers. Peer editing is a strong information literacy skill that creates an awareness in the editor of a problem area and ways to approach it. Editors ask about and respond to choices of problem-solving techniques, opinions, and information application. Their suggestions about writing and presentation help their peers clarify and articulate ideas. While they are editing, students learn new information and how to write better themselves. They take pride in their peers' efforts because they helped make those papers stronger.

The following are techniques we use when we have students edit each other's papers. We have peer editors help the authors by:

1. highlighting redundant material;
2. questioning confusing passages for clarification;
3. suggesting alternative word choices;
4. checking for sentence variety;
5. having adequate supporting details;
6. checking for paragraph organization; and
7. proofing the paper for proper usage, spelling, grammar, and mechanics.

Peer editing supports content learning as well as enhancing the writing and research process. Students working with their writing partners accumulate a wealth of information on topics they might never research but can apply to their lives and to school work. One editor working on the connection of Rachel Carson to marine biology learned about genetics through her peer's paper. Another student coping with chronic asthma gave emotional support to his partner who was investigating her feelings about her adoption. Through peer editing, content knowledge spreads effectively and efficiently from one student to another in the context of the real world. If students choose topics that are personally important, their peers will appreciate the value of the content and tend to remember it.

OPTIONS FOR PRESENTATIONS

One pleasure of the I-Search is its adaptability for use at multiple academic levels. Articles in *English Journal* and other journals for teachers indicate a wide variety of interpretations in using the I-Search. We know teachers who have modified the I-Search for first graders as well as for graduate students. We can use our creativity to transfer this process to any appropriate grade level. We adapt the techniques to the degree of our students' preparedness and add or remove steps according to our objectives. Through our experience, we have discovered that at any level the I-Search is a method that improves information literacy learning as it increases content knowledge, problem solving, and writing abilities.

Teachers and media specialists looking for ways to increase alternative assessment opportunities as well as to teach strong research fundamentals will find the I-Search useful and easy to modify for their purposes. For example, if one of the objectives is to have students acquire computer literacy skills such as presentation techniques, teachers might choose to have them create their final presentation on programs such as Aldus Persuasion, Microsoft PowerPoint, or HyperStudio. Many of the techniques we have discussed are useful in preparing students for this type of final presentation. Our students frequently present an oral discussion of their I-Search as well as write a paper. Students take turns presenting their newly gained knowledge.

The Stearns experience verifies that students who choose personally important topics learn the content during their search, understand how to apply information to their topic, and learn good techniques for using information to problem solve. Many of the Stearns' students chose not to use notes during their oral presentations. Each was confident about her command of the subject and took on the aura of expert. Pride was evident as each underwent interested and reasonably intense questioning by her audience. The students liked the feeling that no one in that room knew as much about the topics being presented as they did. One class actually voted to allow seniors to come hear what they had to say. Having seniors who wanted to listen to their presentations produced excitement rather than fear. These students loved what they had done and were proud of their accomplishments.

To aid students who fear oral presentations or are very shy, we have students form a circle with their chairs and remain seated during the presentation. The speakers also stay seated. If students forget their material, we offer a question or ask other students for a question that usually gets them started again. Telling the story of their search gives them a natural organization that helps them make their material interesting. Most students respond positively to these techniques.

EFFECT ON STUDENTS' LIVES

The best I-Searches continue to affect students' lives long afterwards. One student in particular illustrates this goal. As an asthma sufferer, Jason was shocked to find several articles in weekly news magazines noting an increase in asthma deaths. Could the cause be medication prescribed by doctors? "I knew this was my topic!" Jason wrote in his learning log. "At first I was concerned that the information I would find might scare me a bit, and I would become overly concerned with death. After giving it a lot of consideration, I stuck with it."

Carefully comparing and contrasting facts and opinions from news magazines and the newsletter *Asthma Today*, Jason discovered the real cause of the deaths: human error. He found that sometimes patients were at fault because they failed to follow their doctors' orders. Sometimes the doctors were at fault because they did not give patients adequate explanations of how to care for themselves and use their medications. Jason concluded: "Overall, I believe that most deaths are preventable, and most are the result of carelessness by patient and physician. If people just kept up with the latest medicines and used them properly . . . asthma deaths would greatly be reduced."

But his story did not end with his I-Search. During his interview with his doctor and subsequent office visits, Jason started asking his doctor questions. "My doctor was so impressed with what I knew, he really opened up to me. . . . Now my doctor spends more time with me. He explains my treatment in detail." Jason was not the only student whose search continued beyond the teaching unit. Our underwater welder implemented a plan for gaining skills needed for a challenging career. As mentioned earlier, the student who studied Down's syndrome became an advocate for students with disabilities.

AUTHENTIC ASSESSMENT

We find the I-Search lends itself to authentic assessment. Stripling defines *authentic assessment* as having a real-life context. Authentic assessment has several important components: it is a learning experience for students; it is ongoing throughout the learning process; it is based on real-life content; and it involves reflection by both student and teacher.[1] Authentic assessment means getting feedback in the forms of conferencing, reflection, peer review, and evaluation based on process. The components of the I-Search fit the requirements of authentic assessment organically and effectively. Elements of the authentic assessment definition are found naturally interwoven throughout the I-Search process. Students invest in topics that fit their real-life situations and affect their lives. Reflection continually takes place through learning logs and questioning techniques. Other parts of the process also contribute to an environment that promotes authentic assessment: collaboration, access to tools and resources in and out of the media center, time flexibility, and task management responsibilities. The I-Search requires the kind of feedback that authentic assessment involves.

We can say, therefore, that the I-Search process takes place in an environment of authentic assessment. Students usually have prior knowledge of topics that are related to their lives or their interest areas, which helps them build a natural list of questions they want to answer. This environment also encourages collaboration among students through discussion of their topics, peer questioning, and peer editing of papers. Students help each other solve problems. Logs and conferencing techniques provide students a platform for reflecting and answering their questions. The environment also necessitates collaboration between teacher and media specialist to facilitate the process approach.

Although the I-Search was conceived for college freshmen composition classes as a means to boost writing quality, with modification it lends itself to other types of products required by curriculum objectives. For example, oral presentations, computer presentations, portfolios, as well as the kind of written final products that we've already discussed, can be described as, and fit the definition of, authentic assessment products.

The I-Search encourages use of a broad range of resources from media center materials, to experts, to friends and relations, and to the learner as synthesizer of information. To find information, students rely on electronic databases, interviews, books, periodicals, and the Internet.

The I-Search environment helps students build their task management skills through the flexibility built into the process approach. The students in Maine quickly realized they would have to learn how to organize their time constructively and finish steps in the process at a regular pace to avoid frustration and a poorer quality product at the end. Those who did not accomplish this in the unit under study recognized the problem and expressed the desire to improve on the next assignment. The students who were personally involved with their topics had stronger desires to make steady progress in the research process than those who had "hot" topics. They gave the media specialist and teacher suggestions on how to help their peers make comparable progress. Their suggestions led to improvements in conferencing and questioning to keep track of students who were weaker in this area.

Flexibility is part of the I-Search process and authentic assessment environment. The media specialist and teacher should set aside time for changing course if certain skills need to be retaught or strengthened. Much of the flexibility needed depends on the nature of topics students choose. Some students will rely more on outside resources and interviews, while other students will accomplish much of their research through the media center and interlibrary loan resources.

The real world connection with I-Search topics that is demanded by an authentic assessment environment starts from student choice and continues after the final product is given to the teacher. For the Maine students, it changed relationships with doctors, influenced careers, strengthened the ability to form values, built family relationships, and promoted self-esteem.

The authentic assessment techniques for the I-Search include student reflection; peer review; ongoing conferencing among the teacher, media specialist, and student about student progress; assessment of the process; and the potential of developing rubrics to have the students self-assess the product and experience. Rubrics are scoring guides that describe what varying degrees of mastery or quality look like for each step or component.[2] Some of the questions used for assessment in the Maine I-Search units are listed below. The students believe that the content of the final product belongs to them; thus, our assessment of the content takes a different form in the I-Search. We look at how the facts are used to defend the decision made or solution chosen.

Choosing to assign an I-Search in a specific content area forces some loss of the magic of topic ownership. However, teachers and media specialists can still retain those significant pieces of the process to improve students' sense of research, their knowledge of content, and their writing quality. Depending on the unit's objectives, as much topic choice as possible will help students transfer the process and the content to their lives and future research assignments.

ASSESSMENT SUGGESTIONS

Regardless of the final product's format, we suggest the teacher and media specialist assess content by using levels of Bloom's Taxonomy. We assess process through the following tools: student reflective comments, observations, conferencing, a timeline checklist, and a performance checklist. There are also the traditional means of writing quality assessments for all steps of the process.

Content

These are questions we consider valuable in thinking about assessment of the content.

- Do the learning log and final product display factual accuracy based on a reasonable number of sources? (A "reasonable number" will vary by topic.)
- Are the problem-solving decisions based on information collected during the I-Search?
- Does the content of the learning log and final product demonstrate the student's comprehension of the topic?
- Has the student presented and analyzed more than one approach to solving the problem?
- Has the student applied information as evidence in justifying the solution chosen?
- Has the student presented arguments from several perspectives and synthesized them into the student's own perspective?
- Has the student developed criteria for making a decision on how to solve the problem?

We do not want to judge the specific content the same way we do in traditional term papers. The I-Search creates a different aura around the content. Because of topic ownership, students consider their content to be personal. Thus, we assess students' use of content for problem solving, its accuracy, and its relationship to the problem. Their decision on how to solve their problem is theirs. However, we expect accuracy and justification of their choice. But if they have criteria for solving their problem and can defend it, we accept their solution. The personal nature of the I-Search grants them that privilege.

Process

As a result of the study and student comments, we developed the following questions to help us assess the process and product, all written in a yes or no format. Some of the questions overlap or are ongoing throughout the process, necessitating repetition under other headings. When we use questions to evaluate the whole exercise, we form them into a checklist or we put them in a Likert scale (1: not sufficient, 2: adequate, 3: excellent) to judge the degree of success. To address the important parts of the process, we divide our questions into three categories: *presearch*, *search*, and *presentation*. Depending on the final product, we add questions about *writing quality*.

We stress the importance of sharing this assessment tool with the students at the beginning of the unit to let them know the criteria we will use to evaluate the experience. These questions assist students in checking their progress throughout the I-Search. The questions are particularly useful in the final conference, with the student commenting on progress made in response. Letting students articulate what they think happened solidifies the strengths of the assignment in their minds. Or, we have them finish their learning logs with these questions, stimulating a reflection on their part.

Presearch

- Has the student chosen a personally meaningful topic?
- Does the topic involve decision making and problem solving?
- Does the student display an ability to use a number of strategies to choose a topic—i.e., webbing, index searching, general reading, and interviewing parents and people who know her?
- Does the student understand the topic's limitations and is the student willing to change topics if necessary?
- Can the student create original search questions that move beyond facts and that facilitate solving the problem or making the decision?
- Can the student demonstrate use of information tools, such as electronic indexes and tables of contents, to choose key words that lead to open-ended search questions?
- Can the student focus her topic down to a reasonable number of related questions?
- Does the student show organizational strengths through an ability to prioritize potential topics, search questions, resource choices, and alternative solutions?

Search

- Has the student looked at a sufficient variety of sources or interviewed appropriate contacts/experts in the content area?
- Has the student used a combination of sources, e.g., books, journals, interviews?
- Does the student demonstrate strong information literacy skills in locating, assessing, and using sources?
- Does the student demonstrate an ability to discard irrelevant sources, as evidenced through learning log notes and bibliography?
- Does the student demonstrate use of an organizing technique, such as highlighting and marginal notes, for notetaking?
- Does the learning log show evidence of adequate reflection on gathered information?
- Does the student show an organized approach to solving the problem or making the decision?
- Does the student apply information from a variety of sources for solving the problem or making the decision?

Presentation

- Has the student actually followed through on what the student wanted to accomplish through the search questions?
- Is the paper or presentation clear and well supported?
- Does the paper or presentation reveal clear evidence of effort by the student to carry through the strategies taught through the unit?
- Are the conclusions in the paper or presentation based on information gathered through multiple sources?
- Can the student articulate a personal search strategy to be used in a future assignment?

Writing

One of the strengths of the I-Search is the natural language produced by use of first person. With topic ownership, students write naturally about a topic of concern to themselves. That element might temper several of the following questions. We suggest that the natural flow of the student's language is the most critical factor.

- Does the product demonstrate strong topic development?
- Does the product demonstrate an ability of the student to express thoughts in the first person?

- Does the product present content in a focused, clear, and logical order?
- Does the product provide examples that develop the main points?
- Are the sentences in the final product complete, correct, and varied in structure and length?
- Does the student use appropriate vocabulary?
- Does the student use good spelling, capitalization, punctuation, and paragraphing?

Each of the above questions is based on our experience teaching the I-Search over the last five years. In the study conducted with Martin's students, those who admitted they had skipped some of the process steps also had the most difficulty completing the assignment satisfactorily. The same happened with graduate students. As a result, they did not add some of the most important strategies to their personal research process. This, in turn, resulted in the lack of success in transferring the process and its strategies to other problems or assignments.

We suggest that you develop an assessment format that works best for you. You might want to use the questions to develop a self-assessment rubric for your students to assess themselves, balanced by our opinions. Or, you can work with students to help them create their own criteria for judging certain aspects of the process. We find the more we involve our students with assessment, the more pride they take in the quality of their I-Search.

Finally, we ask our students to reflect on the I-Search unit. Their responses underscore the power of the I-Search process. These are several of the responses we have received:

> I think the I-Search paper was beneficial because it taught me a different way of doing research. Instead of copying down from a book word for word, we read an article and wrote down what we learned and what we thought about the article. And then we wrote about how it applied to us.

> It helped me look more closely at the things I read. Now I understand what I am researching better.

> [I learned] not to take things you see and hear at face value. You have to look deeper into things.

NOTES

1. Barbara K. Stripling, "Learning-centered Libraries: Implications from Research," *School Library Media Quarterly* 23, no. 3 (Spring 1995): 169.

2. Nora Redding, "Assessing the Big Outcomes," in *Assessment and the School Library Media Center*, ed. Carol Collier Kuhlthau (Englewood, CO: Libraries Unlimited, 1994), p. 132.

7 I-SEARCH MANAGEMENT STRATEGIES

Management is critical to the success of the I-Search. Some units are taught within a very short time frame while other units continue over a whole term. Depending on our goals, we guide students in their task management and progress assessment. Evaluation and assessment at critical points during the unit are essential for ensuring good research practice. Students not fully invested in their topic and left on their own tend to skip steps and revert to previous practices and patterns of behavior during research projects. During our interviews of Martin's students, the students requested more supervision and conferences with us to help them learn appropriate task management responsibility. Several of them admitted their problems were a direct result of their neglect of the various steps until the last minute. They fudged on the strategies and backtracked covering steps they did not perform. By reflecting on strategies and process in their learning logs throughout the assignment, students discovered their own habits and poor decisions.

We suggest that you track students closely from step to step to ascertain their success at each stage. Otherwise, some of the freedoms provided by the I-Search give students too much leeway to revert to past unsatisfactory practices; e.g., cutting and pasting and one-source papers written overnight. Many students will find it very difficult to write in the first person without the reflective passages from their learning logs. Their papers become a composite of facts put together in typical fashion without the construction of new ideas or applications. Once off track, it is almost impossible for students working without help to experience the complete process.

Throughout our teaching, two goals always guide us

- to provide adequate time for students to move through the process; and
- to create the atmosphere of cooperation needed to facilitate the process

UNIT TIMELINE

Suggesting a timeline is always a problem with the I-Search—we have so much flexibility in designing how we want to use it. We might want to use the I-Search as a foundation for building research competence. Or, we can use the I-Search as an investigatory method that lends itself to an alternative assignment.

To be successful, a quality I-Search unit takes time. The amount of time depends on the quantity of steps we want to include in the process. It might also depend on the type of assignment, the content area, or the grade level of the students. For example, if we want students to experience all the steps that we have discussed, the unit might last from four to nine weeks, at minimum three. A critical component is the time required for students to reflect on their topics and the information they want to use to solve their problem or make a decision. Thus, the following timeline is suggested as a model.

At Stearns High School, Martin begins her I-Search unit the week before Thanksgiving vacation. She wants students to complete the webbing exercise in time to discuss her web with family members, relatives, and friends during the holiday. Between the Thanksgiving and Christmas holidays, students gather, find, and apply information. They keep detailed records of their actions, thoughts, and feelings in their learning logs. The Christmas holiday gives students time to reflect on the information they have gathered and processed. Sometimes, it is a time for distancing and gaining a fresh perspective on the material. Upon return to school in January, they use their learning logs and any changes they have made during the vacation to write the I-Search paper.

Scheduling I-Search units at the end of the school year produces mixed results. While students appreciate the hands-on learning experiences—i.e., working with information technology, sharing with other students, and conducting interviews associated with the I-Search—the impending end of the school year motivates them to think more about summer vacation than school. Flexibility in scheduling suffers with the approaching closure of the school year. End-of-the-year activities and the frantic rush to complete coursework makes it difficult to modify the schedule.

INDIVIDUALIZED STUDENT TIMELINES

We establish tentative deadlines at various stages of the process to ensure that students stay within the unit's time frame. Each student moves through the process at a slightly different rate.

Dana's story is an example. After the introduction to the I-Search unit, she informed us that she would be absent for the next two days. We were concerned about Dana missing the webbing activity leading to topic selection until we discovered the reason for her absence. Her parents wanted her to attend a private school, but the ultimate decision was up to her. After visiting several schools, Dana would have to make a choice. We quickly revised her timeline. Her topic had obviously chosen her before we assigned the I-Search unit. We immediately moved her to the pre-notetaking phase by suggesting she make a list of questions to ask while visiting private schools. Before returning to school, Dana wrote a narrative of her visit in her learning log. Meanwhile, we rescheduled her introduction to webbing and redefined its purpose. Dana used her web to help her review her life experiences; consider her strengths, weaknesses, and goals; and develop criteria for judging potential schools. She found the school that fit her interests and is now registered there.

Other students encounter temporary obstacles that cause them to fall behind schedule. Most common is the student who must change topics. Steve's research question focused on the purchase of a home computer for his family. At first, he was excited about the topic. He planned to gather information on home computers and share it with his parents. Together, they would decide which one to buy. Then, while doing background reading, Steve confided to us: "I am so confused by my reading. I don't understand half the words in the articles. I need to change my subject." We agreed. In order to move forward, Steve needed to move several steps backwards. With our help, he decided to return to his web, select another topic, complete some general reading, and begin a new pre-notetaking sheet. We worked with Steve to adjust his timeline. The deadline for completing a new pre-notetaking sheet would be extended, but he would have to work a little harder to catch up to the majority in the class.

DEBRIEFING

The timeline provides an overview of the process, steps, and activities and sets potential deadlines; however, flexibility always characterizes our use of time. We constantly modify our I-Search timeline based on input from students. These modifications occur as a result of debriefing.

Throughout the unit, we ask for student input through class sharing and learning logs. Frequently, we begin a class by asking students for a status report. Where are they in the process? What obstacles are they encountering? Do they find any aspect of the process confusing? Do we need to reinforce certain student skills or behaviors before moving to the next step? Are students experiencing feelings of anxiety or frustration? If they are, why? The status report helps us identify time for interventions. Are we moving too fast? Do we need to devote more time to a particular phase in the process? Sometimes we need to provide more practice in the use of a specific strategy. At other times, our strategy is not working and we must seek out an alternative activity.

In addition to class status reports, we skim learning logs during conferences. Sometimes, we work with students while they are involved with their logs during reading and reflecting and completing double-entry drafts. This helps us assist shy students who do not feel comfortable participating in class discussions. Reading learning logs ferrets out students who are not using the steps in a beneficial manner.

We make it a point to debrief students after modeling each strategy or technique. After the lesson on double-entry drafting, for example, we ask them to think about the process. What do you like or dislike about double-entry drafting? How will this strategy help you generate ideas for your learning logs? Responses can alert us that students need more practice before applying the technique independently: "How do I use this to get ideas for my learning log?" Sharing responses can reinforce the value of a technique. For example, students reacted to webbing with these comments: "It helped me find my topic faster." "It made me see more topics."

Listening to students is a critical technique for assessing the I-Search process. It allows us to make necessary modifications and overcome potential obstacles before they become permanent barriers. Sometimes, we find we have to reteach a strategy. When the process is moving smoothly, debriefing sessions give our students and us the reassurance that we are progressing in the right direction.

INTERVENTIONS

Our interventions fall into two categories: full-group interventions devoted to content assessment and individualized interventions that serve a variety of purposes. We have identified specific times in the process when all students need help assessing their topics and level of critical thinking. These interventions occur during webbing, pre-notetaking, and double-entry drafting.

During webbing, we meet with all students to discuss their topics. Is the topic truly choosing them? Or, for the sake of having a topic, are they picking the first subject that seems attractive? Is their lack of experience with self-analysis causing them to miss possible topics from their web? Does the web need more information before a selection is made? We help students generate more ideas and select a personally meaningful subject.

In the case of pre-notetaking and double-entry drafting, the intervention is designed to move all students from lower levels on Bloom's Taxonomy into upper-level critical thinking skills and to provide reassurance. During pre-notetaking conferences, we assist students in developing challenging research questions. Where do their questions fall on the taxonomy? How can they move to a higher level of critical thinking? During double-entry drafting, we intervene through conferencing or by writing comments on their double-entry drafts or in their learning logs.

Individual student interventions involve helping a student develop study skills, matching a student's personal learning style with appropriate activities, and assisting with activities unique to the chosen topic.

Early in the process, we identify the students who need help with organization and sequencing. Jack had an interest in juvenile crime because his friend was in constant trouble with the law. Ironically, shortly after selecting his topic, Jack's friend was arrested again, this time for assaulting a lone teenager. This increased Jack's motivation to find possible solutions to the problem of gang violence and teenage recidivism.

In spite of Jack's interest in both his subject and his collection of related newspaper clippings and magazine articles, we discovered in a conference that his learning log was almost empty. While other students were working on double-entry drafts, he was still trying to decide what information to highlight in his articles. First, we tried to solve the problem by giving Jack a checklist of activities he needed to complete. Still no progress took place. Then a further conference revealed the problem:

> **Teacher:** You have located some excellent articles on juvenile crime and teenage violence. What is your next step?
>
> **Student:** I need to highlight the articles, but I don't know how to do it.
>
> **Teacher:** What information do you want to find through your reading?
>
> **Student:** Why kids do violent things. Why kids keep getting into trouble and how to stop it.
>
> **Teacher:** Then that's what you need to find as you read. When you find information that answers that question, highlight it with your marker.

> **Student:**   That's all there is to it? I thought I needed
> to do more.

Jack was not feigning ignorance to avoid work. He failed to make the connection between research questions and reading for information. Jack also made a false assumption—that if he finds an activity easy, he must be doing something wrong. The conference quickly resolved his misconceptions and the next day, Jack presented us with his highlighted articles. His previous problems also indicated that another intervention on creating double-entry drafts might be in order before moving to the next step.

Some students have organizational problems. An intervention with one of these students resulted in a personalized checklist of activities. When students are overwhelmed by all steps in the process, they hesitate, and their fear of failure becomes an obstacle in itself. It is as if twenty resources have been placed in front of them and they do not know what to do with all the information; much less have they formed a focus for their research. There's no place to start, and they would rather not try than fail in the doing. To overcome this problem in severe cases, a daily intervention might result in individualized lesson plans. We meet with these students at the beginning of the period to determine one specific goal to complete by the end of the period. Near the end of the period, we check their progress. We also help them design a homework assignment that will move them through the next step. Breaking the process into small steps helps these students feel less intimidated. When we combine this strategy with reassurance and praise for each accomplishment, students who feel threatened by the process succeed.

Some intervention involves matching activities with learning styles. Mike was a hands-on and auditory learner who wanted to learn about underwater welding for his career. We helped him locate a video on welding which gave him background information on his subject. He also used a computer program in the guidance office to obtain a printout of two technical colleges offering training in underwater welding. These sources helped Mike create questions for an interview with the welding instructor at the high school. We suggested he use an audiocassette recorder to tape the interview with the instructor's approval. After the interview, Mike listened to the tape and found passages for his double-entry drafts. His resource investigation and reflection strategies matched his learning style.

Finally, interventions sometimes include specialized training. Our student studying Down's syndrome received permission to videotape an interview with her Down's friend and his family.

Melissa already had training in running her family's video camera, but she needed some pointers on how to film the interview.

Sharon was studying violence in high school football. She wanted to survey members of the football team. We helped her design questions for the survey. This activity was a good opportunity to involve her math teacher, too. We suggested that Sharon ask him for help in analyzing her data and deriving her statistics.

Interventions have many purposes and take many formats. They require class time, planning, and management strategies. After our first experiences with the I-Search taught us the necessity of interventions, we now make sure to include time in our unit.

HOMEWORK

Although we devote many class periods to individualized work on the I-Search process, homework is still a necessary component of the process. At home, students conference with parents, guardians, close relatives, and/or adult friends about their webbing diagrams and topic selection. During the pre-notetaking stage, students bring home computer printouts and photocopies of articles so that they can skim them and create questions. Students use time at home to highlight print materials and plan and conduct interviews. Later, homework creates the time to reflect on double-entry drafts written in class; students reread their responses at home and then write learning log entries. A common homework activity is reflecting on the day's class work. What were their actions, feelings, and thoughts for the day? We also check on students' use of time at home during conferences by asking them to show us their work or explain how they are using their time outside of class.

TAKING A BREAK

I-Search units are intense and require a commitment of time and energy. Media specialists and teachers who collaborate on such a unit need planning and debriefing time before and after classes. During class, they need time to meet individually with students. Students who select personally meaningful topics often have an emotional commitment as well. As students deal with topics such as divorce, adoption, illness, and death, they frequently need support in addressing the issues for their investigation. Such topics must have parental permission and support, and, frequently, their involvement.

At times during the I-Search unit, we and our students feel overwhelmed. This is the time for a break. While students are gathering or processing information outside of school, we sometimes use class time to read and discuss short stories, cast and read a one-act play, or experiment with writing poetry. We design several one- or two-day curriculum activities into the time frame when we think they will be needed. Not only does this provide a break for students dealing with emotional issues, but it also provides us with "catch up" time.

COOPERATIVE LEARNING

Group activity facilitates the sharing of content and process for I-Searching. The Maine students have experience in writing groups, a form of cooperative learning. Our groups consist of four or five students. To promote peer teaching, we mix students with different strengths and abilities. For example, we place a student who is good at generating details in a group with a second student who has excellent organizational stills. A third student in the group is skillful at spotting logical and illogical arguments while a fourth is a natural leader. In short, each student complements the others. At various stages of the process, we have students meet with the members of their groups. Students take turns reading excerpts from their learning logs, or, at the end of the unit, drafts of their I-Search papers. When each reading is completed, listeners in the group comment on the contents.

Following Macrorie's suggestions for peer editing, which emphasizes a non-threatening atmosphere, we train students to ask questions instead of making critical comments. The following are some question starters that address the issues of content and process:

Content Questions:
1. I am confused by _____. Can you explain it to me?
2. What other details support _____?
3. Can you think of another way of arranging your key points?
4. What is the main idea?
5. What are the opposing viewpoints to your opinion?

Process Questions:
1. How will you find more information? What other resources might you consult?
2. What problem do you face here? How will you overcome it? Have you tried _____?
3. How current is this material?
4. Do you think the author is biased?
5. What is your next step?

Having students pose questions instead of making critical comments maintains a positive atmosphere and helps the authors explore possibilities. Ownership of the writing stays with the author who can choose to accept or ignore the suggestions.

We use a "fly on the wall" approach to facilitating sharing groups. We move from group to group listening to discussions and intervening when necessary. Interventions include keeping students on task by reminding them of the group's purpose or procedures, encouraging a quiet or shy student to ask a question, and reminding students who dominate the discussion to share their time with others.

SHARING RESPONSIBILITIES

The I-Search presents an excellent opportunity to practice collaborative planning and teaching. It provides a natural opening for the media specialist and teacher together to plan a unit, design both content and information literacy objectives, plan activities, share the teaching, assess student learning, and evaluate the unit. At first, more responsibilities are placed on the partner who is adept at process teaching. Gradually, as the other partner gains understanding of the process approach, they share responsibilities. The demands of sharing also depend on the depth of the unit conducted. If the I-Search is used for a short activity, one person is generally capable of handling the teaching and assessment. An extended unit requires both being available. Class size also makes a difference.

We have conducted workshops on the I-Search process at state and national conferences. A frequent question asked at these presentations involves the division of labor. How do the media specialist and teaching partner share responsibilities? We emphasize working as a team to conduct these lessons. While modeling the webbing activity, one partner questions the interviewee while the other records the responses. A similar organizational structure is used for the pre-notetaking demonstration. For example, the media specialist gives a lesson on how to use key words to write research questions. Then the teacher has the class brainstorm questions for a sample topic using a page from an index reproduced on an overhead. The media specialist records the student responses on the blackboard. Together, they conduct a follow-up discussion on how to evaluate the questions for critical thinking at the upper level of Bloom's hierarchy. As a result of this sharing of labor, students perceive teacher and media specialists as a team with equal authority. This helps to establish the atmosphere needed for the sharing of other responsibilities such as conferencing and assessment.

Both media specialist and teacher should try to meet periodically with each student. This requires coordination so that individual students do not receive conflicting messages. Together, the two review conferences and give each other a brief assessment of student progress. Their debriefing time is for sharing and problem-solving, with joint planning helping to solidify their partnership. The sharing creates a chemistry which facilitates new ideas for unit instruction.

Not all partnerships involve an equal division of labor, particularly when one person initiates the I-Search. Part of it depends on who the process advocate is. One scenario might have the teacher taking more responsibility for the I-Search and the media specialist concentrating on information skills. Or, at other times, the media specialist becomes the catalyst for change and promotes I-Search to the teacher.

At Stearns High School, upper-level teachers saw a disparity between students who had experienced I-Search and students who had not in terms of comfort levels and understanding of research strategy. They pushed for the I-Search for all students. That meant that some non-process teachers became involved with the I-Search unit. At first, the media specialist took most of the responsibility for implementing the unit. The teachers learned with the students. After experiencing the process, they gradually took over responsibilities for content and writing, and shared the conferencing. These relationships grew more collaborative with the completion of each unit.

PERSONALIZING THE PROCESS

Sharing sample learning log entries and model I-Search papers inspires students and increases their understanding of the nature of the process and product. Ultimately, each student's I-Search is unique to her personal experience. The same is true for media specialists and teachers who develop their own strategies and techniques that apply to their environment. What we present in this book has worked for us as we increase our knowledge of the I-Search experience each time we teach it. We encourage personalizing the process to match student needs with the ingredients that work best for you. Our experiences can be a model.

Learning how to teach the I-Search is a process in itself. As we look back at our experiences, the mistakes and problems seem minor compared to the enthusiasm of most of our students. From the beginning, we involved our students in our learning process. We told them that they were part of an important experiment. We needed their input. They would evaluate our teaching strategies. What worked? What did not work?

Our students appreciated being involved in the decision-making process and knowing that their opinions counted. They valued recounting their experiences and what they had learned; it made them feel important. Their responses were rewarding. One shy student who participated in our research study had at first refused to be interviewed until her mother, a frequent substitute in the Stearns media center, persuaded her to participate. Reflecting on her experience in the interview gave her unexpected courage to voice her opinions publicly. One year later in a school-sponsored workshop designed to involve teachers, students, parents, and community leaders in establishing the school's educational goals, she found strength to express her opinion about the I-Search experience: "It's the only time someone asked for my opinion."

Giving students a vested interest in the process as well as the product can have a ripple effect on their lives.

8 INSERVICE TRAINING

"The key to student growth is educator growth."[1] When you discover the I-Search's potential, you will want to share it with colleagues. The quickest way to do that is through a staff development workshop. As the workshop leader, you will benefit from having taught I-Search units or from having a comprehensive understanding of the process approach. Your knowledge of the components of the I-Search process and its strategies and experience working with students on I-Search units will be invaluable. You will be prepared to anticipate and answer questions from staff and solve problems that arise during the workshops.

FOUR COMPONENTS OF INSERVICE TRAINING

I-Search workshops can take a variety of formats depending on the time available for inservice training. Before deciding on the type of program, consider the components of the inservice training process. Joyce and Showers identify these as the following: theory, demonstration, practice, and peer coaching. The first component consists of exploring current theories through reading, attending lectures and workshops, and discussing with colleagues what is learned. The second component involves the demonstration or modeling of a skill or activity, while the third involves practicing the skill or activity under simulated conditions. The final component is peer coaching: Teachers and media specialists who are implementing new units or innovative teaching practices coach each other in solving problems and addressing questions.[2]

Research reveals that the most successful form of inservice training consists of a combination of all of the above components.[3] Consequently, time becomes a critical factor. The more time devoted to inservice training in I-Searching, the more components you can incorporate into the training. The greater the number of components, the greater the teachers' and media specialists' ability to implement I-Search units with success.

ONE-HOUR SESSIONS

Sessions with an hour time limit can introduce teachers, media specialists, and administrators to the I-Search process and its strategies. The stories of some of your searchers are very appropriate for hooking listeners in an introductory presentation. With the use of overheads and handouts, you can review the theory behind the I-Search process, present an overview of its steps, and describe briefly the corresponding activities.

The second format focuses on modeling and simulating one activity related to the I-Search. For example, an hour presentation easily lends itself to training teachers and media specialists in the use of double-entry drafts. You can apply the same techniques that you find in Chapter Five of this book. During the presentation, the two-day training session for students is compressed into an hour. This is sufficient time for media specialists and teachers to watch a demonstration of how to write a double-entry draft, see some examples, practice writing two of their own drafts, share the results with other participants, and participate in a short debriefing session that allows for comments and questions.

In terms of transferring skills, informal follow-ups to the introductory presentations reveal mixed results. Some teachers and media specialists with a background in the process approach, such as English and language arts teachers with experience in process writing, included the I-Search in their curriculum. Other teachers and media specialists lacking experience with the process approach needed additional exposure to feel comfortable with the process before they initiated their first unit. Conversely, after a session that modeled and simulated one of the I-Search strategies, more people were able to assimilate the I-Search into their teaching.

THE TWO-DAY WORKSHOP

A two-day workshop allows for more intensive training in the I-Search process and permits the integration of the four components of inservice training into the programming. We assisted a regional group of media specialists in Maine in planning and implementing a two-day I-Search workshop. Each media specialist attending the workshop brought a teacher interested in collaborating on an I-Search unit. The workshop was conducted in a media center with a good print collection and a computer network providing access to a variety of electronic resources. During the two days, each team was taken through a shortened, modified simulation of the I-Search process. The two-day workshop presented in this book is a modification of the Maine workshop.

Our assessment of the Maine workshop reveals that location in a good media center is critical in giving participants an opportunity to start developing their own I-Search units. Having the teacher work with a media specialist as a team also encourages collaborative planning of research process instruction once the workshop is finished. When both partners receive the training together, their understanding of the process is mutual and supportive. They practice peer coaching with each other.

The program outlined below stresses our choice of four major elements taught with the I-Search:

- Choosing a topic through webbing.
- Finding a focus through pre-notetaking.
- Reflective writing in learning logs.
- Analyzing and evaluating information through double-entry drafting.

During the two-day period, each morning and afternoon session is devoted to modeling and simulating one of these activities. At the end of the institute, we encourage participants to complete an I-Search on their own and we make arrangements for peer coaching for people who plan to implement I-Search units.

The workshop also includes explanations of theory and strategies, modeling by the facilitators, practice by participants, and peer coaching through conferencing and monitoring. We use debriefing sessions to give workshop participants a chance to voice their concerns and present problems for the group to solve. Debriefing is important for helping participants discuss how to adapt and modify the I-Search for different grade levels and ability groups. Through debriefing, the facilitators are able to discover what interventions are needed with participants and to make adjustments in the schedule and activities.

PRE-CONFERENCE ASSIGNMENT

To provide a place for storing handouts and materials created during the workshop, we ask participants to bring a loose-leaf notebook. We pre-punch our handouts so that they can be incorporated easily into the notebook. This notebook is also a good place to store materials created at a later date as they implement their I-Search units.

SCHEDULE FOR THE TWO-DAY WORKSHOP

Day One—Morning

We introduce ourselves and the purpose of the workshop by telling I-Search stories from our teaching experiences. Then we ask participants to recall and reflect in their notebooks, which will become their learning logs, on their past research and learning experiences. We give them ten minutes for several short writing prompts that we call "ice-breakers" to stimulate reflective thinking about their experiences. Sharing experiences recounted in these prompts opens the lines of communication among participants.

Ice-breaker Prompts

1. Think back to when you were a student. How did you react when your teacher said, "Your next assignment is a research project"?

2. Describe both a positive and negative research experience you remember from elementary, junior, or senior high school. List five things you did when you were assigned one of these research projects. Describe your reactions to these projects. What emotions did you have?

3. Describe a moment in or out of school that was a meaningful learning experience. What did you learn? Why was it meaningful?

For small groups, we have participants sit in a circle and share their experiences with the entire group. For larger groups, participants can divide into groups of five or six and informally share their experiences. We conduct a debriefing session at the end of the twenty-minute sharing time to make the connection between the positive experiences and the information processing learning theory. This theory essentially states that people work to make sense of the information that they collect through their senses. They apprehend, structure, categorize, and store it for future use in ways that make the most meaning to them.[4] We design this exercise to give participants connections among the workshop's activities, curriculum issues, and information problem-solving needs.

The sharing of personal experiences related to learning helps participants move to the next activity: using a webbing diagram to discover topics related to a personal need for information. Using one of the workshop participants or an outside volunteer as the subject, we model the creation of the personal experience webbing diagram. The activity follows the same procedure used with students as explained in Chapter Three. Following the mapping, we discuss how participants can adapt or modify the webbing technique to meet the needs of students in various grade levels. For example, senior high students have more life experiences and will have more intricate maps than elementary students.

Some participants might also want some ideas on how to improve questioning strategies to elicit more detailed responses from their students. We tell them, for example, that they can encourage students to have parents/guardians, close relatives, and friends recall important events and people in their lives. Employing the technique of open-ended questions, we will ask a student: "Tell me the story about that experience."

From that story, we elicit from her the elements that interest her the most, and ask what she knows and might want to know about those elements.

After the discussion, participants work on their own webbing diagrams and practice the questioning strategies with each other. This exercise simulates how they will interact with their students and helps them select one or two topics from their webs for an I-Search. For their short I-Search experience, we stress that their topic choice will be limited by time constraints and the availability of resources at the workshop site.

Day One—Afternoon
We begin the afternoon session by having participants reflect on their morning experiences by writing in their learning logs. What did they learn? What are their feelings about the I-Search process so far? What questions or problems need to be answered? Then, we have participants share responses to help each other solve problems and answer questions. If necessary, we make adjustments in the schedule and revisit the webbing activity if participants are confused.

Next, we introduce the "accordion" exercise discussed in Chapter Three. In this exercise, participants write questions in response to the topic that they would like the researcher to answer and share their reactions to their peers' questions about their own topics. We explain how this strategy might be used to choose their general topic and to begin determining a focus.

Having one of the participants talk through her topic gives us a chance to model writing questions for the pre-notetaking sheet. We follow the same procedures we use with students. During the debriefing discussion following the modeling, we stress connections with Bloom's Taxonomy and discuss how to use the action verbs in our chart to create research questions reflecting upper-level critical thinking skills.

Assuming topics arise from genuine personal need, the participants probably have prior knowledge of their topics. From that prior knowledge they can decide what they want to know and fill in their own pre-notetaking sheets. If the topic is a new one for them, they can use the media center's resources to create the questions for the "What I Want to Know" column. In both cases, the "What I Want to Know" column generates a focus for the topic through the questions. After doing this procedure, participants should have four or five related questions to guide their research.

For the final afternoon activity, participants pair up for peer conferencing. During the conference, they practice using Bloom's Taxonomy and the action verbs to help each other revise their research questions so that the questions reflect upper-level critical thinking.

Day Two—Morning
Participants begin the morning session on the second day making revisions, as they see fit, on parts of their pre-notetaking sheets. They assess the pre-notetaking sheet as an activity for generating relevant topics, finding a focus, and creating research questions. This assessment gives them a vested interest in these activities for their own use later. Before they continue, they should be able to express their opinions again on any

modifications they think would contribute to these activities for their purposes. Reflective time is always constructive.

The remainder of the morning is devoted to the most important tool for selecting, evaluating, and using information: the double-entry draft. We follow the same training procedure described in Chapter Five. After completing the first double-entry draft for their personal I-Search, participants work in groups of three or four to read their double-entry drafts and give feedback on each other's responses. They use questions at the upper level of Bloom's Taxonomy to challenge each other's thinking, and eventually share their work as a team with the whole group. This activity stresses peer coaching and facilitates the greatest amount of learning for this technique.

Day Two—Afternoon
We have participants create double-entry drafts for information from resources they locate in the media center or from interviewing their peers. Participants seek advice from each other when problems arise. We monitor participants' progress by listening to them as they work with each other. We are prepared to conduct interventions if participants cannot resolve their problems or if they are off-task.

When they are satisfied their double-entry drafts reflect their perspective on the information they have collected, they enter their responses into their learning logs. If the original information needs citing, they note where they obtained the information in the form required by the assignment: e.g., full or short bibliographic citation style. We demonstrate, by using their entries that the learning log containing these reflections is the primary source for students writing their final papers in the first person. The reflective exercise required by the double-entry draft and learning log boosts students' ability to retain information in their own words in long-term memory.

Finally, we address the issue of implementation by asking participants to contribute ideas on implementing an I-Search unit in their school. What first step would they take to make their I-Search unit a reality? If a number of participants contribute, they will go home with ideas on how to approach this key aspect of the experience. This final activity challenges each participant to initiate her own unit.

Before leaving the workshop, we help participants form a support network with other participants. They select a means of sharing their experiences as they create their own I-Search units. Some participants make plans to communicate through e-mail while others use telephone calls or on-site visits. Setting up a network among the participants will create support for when everyone goes home; everyone will have contact with other people who have experienced the same training. They work as a team to solve problems that develop as they implement their own I-Search units and share their successes. This support serves as an opportunity for continued peer coaching and sharing of ideas.

FIVE-DAY WORKSHOP

Because of its length, we list below the activities we think should be included in a five-day workshop. What we actually do depends on the number of participants we have, their background experience and grade levels, the location of the workshop, the availability of resources for a short I-Search experience, the strategies we want to include, and the final product we want to emphasize for the I-Search. For example, if a school district wants to consider the I-Search as a way of incorporating technology use by students, we might include a short section modeling I-Search products created with presentation software. Following is a possible breakdown of sessions and their contents.

Session One

1. Introduce facilitators and participants.
2. Review the goals for the workshop, explain the I-Search process, and review the agenda for the five-day period. If possible, include student stories to motivate participants.
3. Describe use of participants' notebooks as learning logs.
4. Have participants respond to the Ice-breaker prompts in their notebooks.
5. Have participants share the experiences described in their Ice-breaker prompts.
6. Use key ideas from their experiences to explain the connection between learning theory and positive learning experiences.

Session Two

1. Explain the concept of "the topic chooses you" and relate it to the topic selection process.
2. Model the webbing activity used as a tool for topic selection.
3. Have participants create their own webs.
4. Have participants conference with peers about webs.
5. Have each participant select and prioritize possible topics.
6. Have participants reflect on webbing as an activity for generating topics in their learning logs.
7. Debrief the webbing activity by having participants share the responses from their learning logs.
8. Have participants skim and scan potential resources to determine the scope and personal level of interest in their potential topics.

9. Conduct interventions and individualized conferences with participants having problems with topic selection.
10. Have participants share their topics with the group.

Session Three

1. Review the steps in the presearch process.
2. Explain the three strategies you will use to complete the pre-notetaking sheet:
   - The "accordion" activity to generate research questions related to personal interest
   - The use of key words and names to write research questions
   - The use of classification skills to group together related questions and to determine a focus
3. Demonstrate the "accordion" activity.
4. Have the participants complete the "accordion" activity and add the relevant questions generated to their pre-notetaking sheets.
5. Demonstrate use of key words and names to create more research questions for pre-notetaking sheets. Show how to classify questions by finding several related questions to serve as a focus.
6. Have participants use print and electronic indexes, abstracts, and tables of contents to find key words and then use those key words to create research questions to add to their pre-notetaking sheets. Then have them select several related questions to use as their focus.
7. Review Bloom's Taxonomy as a tool for assessing students' level of critical thinking. Model an intervention designed to create questions reflecting more complex levels of critical thinking.
8. Have participants work with a partner to simulate interventions by assessing and conferencing about their pre-notetaking sheets. Then have them revise their research questions using input from their partners.

Session Four

1. Explain the purpose of general background reading.
2. Have participants do general background reading.
3. Have participants read without notetaking. Set aside time for them to note the most memorable passages and their reactions in their learning logs.
4. Have participants revise their pre-notetaking sheets

based on what they learned from general background reading and reading without notetaking.

5. Have participants reflect on the pre-notetaking process as a whole in their learning logs.

6. Share the responses on pre-notetaking from the learning logs.

Session Five

1. Have participants familiarize themselves with their resources.

2. Have participants plan for interviews.

3. Have participants create a plan of action for using resources.

4. Have participants highlight text and add marginal notes to print materials using the guidelines in Chapter Four.

5. Explain and model double-entry drafting using newspaper articles according to the guidelines explained in Chapter Five.

6. Have participants complete a double-entry draft for the first highlighted resource included in their action plan. Then have them write and reflect in a learning log entry using the information from the double-entry draft.

7. Have participants conference with peers about the double-entry draft and corresponding learning log. Have them focus on using Bloom's Taxonomy both to assess their partner's level of critical thinking and to make suggestions.

8. Have participants reflect on double-entry drafting in their learning logs.

9. Debrief the responses on double-entry drafting from the learning logs.

Session Six

1. Demonstrate how to use the learning log as a tool for creating a final product.

2. Have participants create a web or outline of the evolution of their search from topic choice to final learning log entry.

3. Have participants translate the web or outline into a brief paper.

4. Describe the process of peer editing.

5. Have participants work with partners to edit their papers.

Session Seven

1. Give participants the assessment questions contained in Chapter Six.
2. Have participants work with partners to assess their papers and to discuss the I-Search process.
3. Have participants write a final reflective statement on the workshop's activities and the I-Search process as they intend to use it.
4. Have participants share those statements in a debriefing session.

Because a five-day session requires considerable flexibility in time commitments for each activity, we have purposely avoided specifying the timeline. But we advise constructing a potential timeline to help gauge progress during the workshop.

NOTES

1. Bruce Joyce and Beverly Showers, *Student Achievement through Staff Development: Fundamentals of School Renewal* (White Plains, NY: Longman, 1995), p. xv.
2. Joyce and Showers, p. 110.
3. Joyce and Showers, p. 112.
4. Dolores Fadness Tadlock, "SQ3R—Why It Works, Based on an Information Processing Theory of Learning," *Journal of Reading* 22, no. 2 (November 1978): 111.

9 CONNECTIONS TO INFORMATION LITERACY

DEFINITION OF INFORMATION LITERACY

We are strong believers in the I-Search for a number of reasons. The components of the I-Search touch on all facets of the definition published in the California Media and Library Educators' handbook on information literacy describing an information literate person:

An information literate person *accesses* information.

- Recognizes the need for information
- Recognizes that accurate and complete information is the basis for intelligent decision making
- Formulates questions based on information needs
- Identifies potential sources of information
- Develops successful search strategies
- Accesses print and technology-based sources of information
- Is a competent reader

An information literate person *evaluates* information.

- Establishes authority
- Determines accuracy and relevance
- Recognizes point of view and opinion versus factual knowledge
- Rejects inaccurate and misleading information
- Creates new information to replace inaccurate or missing information as needed

An information literate person *uses* information.

- Organizes information for practical application
- Integrates new information into an existing body of knowledge
- Applies information in critical thinking and problem solving.[1]

This list is a form of process itself that allows scaffolding from level to level and provides the structure for a process unit. It fits very well with the I-Search strategies we have described. Matching the I-Search process with the California list assures us that students who undertake the I-Search do get a solid information literacy experience.

THE I-SEARCH AS AN INFORMATION LITERACY EXPERIENCE

Because of topic ownership in the I-Search, students develop almost a psychological need for information. Their problems require answers for them, rather than for us, thus providing an intrinsic motivation. When they find opposing viewpoints, they then have a need to discover the most accurate and valid information. Their research questions become the instrument to focus the search where their hunger for information is strongest. They require research strategies allowing them to satisfy their appetites. Part of that appetite is a desire to process information through the senses. Therefore, the I-Search process lends itself to students using multiple sources of information, regardless of format. These sources can include information from reading, listening, talking, and, depending on the topic, touching, tasting, and smelling. The I-Search presents opportunities for students to use interviews, opinions, and personal experiences, as well as formal resources.

The strategies presented in this book help students make sense of content and help them process content through reflection and the comparing and contrasting of information for authority, accuracy, and relevancy. The use of double-entry drafts in their learning logs gives them a tool to create new information that fits their problem-solving appetite.

The I-Search requires student authors to organize their information through the search story. A past relationship with the topic provides a solid foundation for adding new knowledge. That is the difference between students who choose topics related to their needs and those who choose more academic topics. We all want to tell our stories. There is an intrinsic motivation to announce our discoveries and share meaningful personal experiences. As a result, writing about the topic and the story of the search automatically pushes the I-Search onto a higher level of thinking than a mere collection of facts pasted together.

The I-Search develops students' ability to participate in all of the areas listed by the California educators by taking them through the steps in the process suggested in the preceding chapters. The value of these steps as a research process is their adaptability to whatever need the students have, as long as the students retain ownership of their topics and learn the strategies essential to filling their needs. When topic ownership is removed or lessened by designating subject area topics, even where choice is given, the process still works but transferability of strategies is not as certain and intrinsic motivation is not guaranteed. Once students have learned that they can satisfy a personal hunger for information, they will want to satisfy it again. When they do not own that hunger, they do not have as intense an investment in trying to sate it.

CONNECTION WITH OTHER PROCESSES

The I-Search interconnects with Murray's explanation of the writing process that we have previously discussed[2], and SQ3R, an effective reading process.[3] The I-Search follows the same organizational steps defined through the information processing theory of learning that underpins SQ3R. Tadlock says, "Humans inherently strive to 'make sense' out of their world—to reduce their uncertainty concerning the nature of the world."[4] Humans work to make sense of the information that they collect through their senses. They apprehend, structure, categorize, and store information for future use in ways that make the most meaning to them.[5]

When processes interweave, they gain strength from each other and provide the student with a stronger foundation for achievement as an information literate person. Instead of teaching processes, individual research steps, or individual skills isolated from their connections to writing and reading, the I-Search connects all three. The difference is the emphasis on topic choice which provides the stimulus for involvement with the process and ownership of the content. Rather than having students concentrate on fitting their topics into a series of steps that have to be followed, as has been traditionally taught, the I-Search provides a natural exposure to strategies that help students solve their problems. As our study indicated, students may not be able to define the research process verbally when they are finished, but they are able to describe the steps they will repeat for the next assignment they get, or the next problem they need to solve, or the next decision they have to make. They have assimilated the process into their personal method of learning.

Although students may begin with a grade motivation, many soon forget grades and concentrate on the problem. They write to solve their problem or answer an information need. Because the I-Search includes reflection on search strategies in the learning log and the story of their search as part of the final product, they can articulate the most useful steps they took to find and use information. This part of the process boosts their ability to store the steps they have taken within their long-term memory. They also know the steps that did not prove successful and why. In addition, these reflections give instructors an evaluation of where the unit needs improvement and where it is working well.

It may seem to the reader that we have given an overwhelming amount of space to topic choice; however, our study of the Maine high school students provides us with the evidence of its value in teaching students a research process. Remember the student whose grandmother had died of Amyotrophic Lateral Sclerosis, causing the student to worry about her own health? How about the student who carved out a career in underwater welding for himself? Or the student who formed a productive and enlightening relationship with his doctor about his asthma treatments? There were many students in this category who directly applied the information gained through their searches to their life situations.

In contrast, the students who searched the Bermuda Triangle, dreams, UFOs, etc., were interested in varying degrees in their topics, but not as involved in what they did. Their eyes did not sparkle when they described their experiences. They were quicker to point out problems, in greater quantity, with their research. Their task management techniques gave them trouble as they lost time in class to socializing and straying off task. They exhibited less command of their topics and less pleasure in the results. They used grades as their main motivation, or expressed less sense of caring about the grade they received. They had a more difficult time writing in the first person because they had not invested themselves in their topics. Having no relationship with UFOs or the Bermuda Triangle, these students developed only a passing interest in their "hot" topics.

In short, good topic choice corrals the student's intrinsic motivation to accomplish the research in order to answer a need. Mike, our underwater welder, told us in an interview, "If I pick my topic, I [will] do a good job on it. If you pre-pick a topic for me, and I don't like the topic, I'm not going to do a good job. It's something I'm not interested in. I have to be interested in it to do it." One of the most troublesome tasks in giving research assignments is forcing students to take on topics in which they have little interest and about which even less knowledge. Yes, it is important to give them subject area content knowledge but not when teaching the research process is the main focus. During the I-Search, they receive *life* content knowledge.

NOTES

1. California Media and Library Educators Association, *From library skills to information literacy: A handbook for the 21st century* (Castle Rock, CO: Hi Willow Research and Publishing, 1994), pp. 2–3.
2. Donald M. Murray, "Writing as Process: How Writing Finds Its Own Meaning," in *Learning by Teaching: Selected Articles on Writing and Teaching* (Portsmouth, NH: Heinemann, 1982), p. 23.
3. Dolores Fadness Tadlock, "SQ3R—Why It Works, Based on an Information Processing Theory of Learning," *Journal of Reading* 22, no. 2 (November 1978): 110–112.
4. Ibid., p. 111.
5. Ibid.

10 SUMMARY

The I-Search complements the other information seeking and research processes available. It includes strategies that help students complete all the steps suggested in current library and information skills instruction models. In addition, it injects a sense of ownership to the process. Students are encouraged to reflect on the strategies that help their projects succeed, and to choose alternatives for strategies that are less helpful. The I-Search's connections with Bloom's Taxonomy ensures its staying power as a viable instructional method for teaching critical thinking through the research process.

What we like most about the I-Search is its naturalness and relevancy to student lives and information needs. Students in our research study who chose personally relevant topics did not hesitate to express delight with what they had accomplished and how much it meant to them. One young student not living with his Native American father discovered more of his heritage when his father and sister shared family and tribal history. Another student developed a healthy skepticism towards advertising claims about fishing equipment. He wanted to catch large fish through the ice, but he knew he would have to test the equipment himself to verify the claims. Most students with personal topics agreed with the student who reported that, "It helped me look more closely at the things I read to see if the authors agreed, or if the statements were just theories or real facts. I think it taught me a lot about how to put things in my perspective, to understand what I am responding to better." On the other hand, students who had chosen more typical school topics reacted similarly to the following statement from a student: "[My topic] was one that only abstractly affected me. It was a lot harder at times to have an opinion on things."

Does the I-Search transfer to other assignments? According to the sophomore, junior, and senior class subject teachers at Stearns High School, it does. When they gave research assignments, they could tell which students had completed an I-Search unit. These students knew immediately how to start their project and what steps to take. Their task management strategies were apparent. Students who had not done an I-Search floundered until the teacher could take them through the steps one-by-one. Teachers found they could raise their research expectations of I-Search experienced students and could design a broader array of activities. Students entered their classes with more confidence and willingness to research for the sake of gaining new knowledge. Their teachers found it a refreshing change. We hope you will, too.

Breivik and Gee claim that, "transferability is the essence of information literacy."[1] We agree. The I-Search seems to do just that. Finally, Kuhlthau stresses that students benefit from a sequential, K-12 library media program based on the process approach to information literacy. Students profit because they come to understand their personal research process.[2] Kuhlthau explains:

> They learn that thinking, reflecting, and mulling are an important part of learning from information; that uncertainty is not only okay, it is the beginning of all learning. They take the initiative to find out and the responsibility for telling others. These are basic skills for the information age.[3]

This quote summarizes what the I-Search accomplishes. With the strategies we have included, the I-Search process demands that students participate in the activities descibed in the quote. It is a research process based on the information processing theory of learning and is intimately connected with the other critical learning processes taught in reading and writing classes. It includes all of the steps described in the processes currently available as instructional models for teaching information skills. If you are a process teacher and advocate, you will find it fits naturally into your instructional plans. If you have not followed process teaching, take the time to learn and perfect how you want to teach the I-Search. Be patient with your units and build on them each year. It is worth the investment for the research foundation it gives students as they complete their studies.

NOTES

1. Patricia Senn Breivik and E. Gordon Gee, *Information Literacy: Revolution in the Library* (New York: American Council on Education/ Macmillan, 1989), p. 47.
2. Carol C. Kuhlthau, "Information Search Process: A Summary of Research and Implications for School Library Media Programs," *School Library Media Quarterly* 18, no. 1 (Fall 1989): 22.
3. Ibid.

APPENDIXES

APPENDIX A: COLLABORATING THROUGH CONFERENCING

WHEN, WHAT AND HOW

Conferencing can occur at any time in the process, especially when a student is confused or has encountered an obstacle. Nevertheless, there are stages in the process when it should probably be done with all students. These times are listed below. Both media specialist and teacher share responsibility for conferencing with students. During the conferences, other students are working on their learning logs, reading about their subjects at their desks, or using resources in the library. Possibly, students trained in peer conferencing could meet with other students in the class while the teacher and media specialist hold individual conferences.

During conferences the media specialist and teacher *ask questions and give students choices*. Students solve their own problems and draw their own conclusions—under the teacher's and media specialist's guidance who avoid "telling" them what to do.

Students *follow up each conference by writing in their learning logs*. They summarize the discussion and react to its contents. This way, they don't forget what has been discussed. When the teacher and media specialist read their logs, they can tell if students understand the key points that evolved through the discussion.

Not enough time to conference? Carry on dialogues in students' learning logs. Each night take a few learning logs home and write questions in the margins. Students can answer the questions in their logs.

TIMES TO CONFERENCE AND SAMPLE QUESTIONS: PRE-NOTETAKING

Goal:
To help student
find a focus

I. After the selection of a potential topic
    A. Content questions
        1. Why did you select this topic?
        2. What do you already know about the subject?
        3. Can you tell me more about _____ ?
        4. Did you know that _____ ?
    B. Process questions
        1. Do you think you have a broad or a narrow topic? Why?
        2. What will be your next step?

Goal: to help students formulate "what they don't know" questions

II. After drafting questions on Pre-Notetaking Sheet
    A. Content questions
        1. What other questions might you ask?
        2. Have you created at least one question from each one of your key words?
    B. Process questions
        1. What strategy can you use to generate more research questions?
        2. What is the secret to writing a good research question?
        3. What indexes and tables of contents have been the most helpul when creating questions? Why?
        4. What obstacles have you encountered? How do you plan to overcome them?
        5. What is your next step?

Goal: to determine questions for their "Questions I will Answer through My Research" column and to formulate the central research question

III. While revising questions on Pre-Notetaking Sheet
    A. Content
        1. Are you satisfied with your central research question? Is it an accurate picture of what you will show through your research? Justify your answer.
        2. Do all of the questions to guide your research support your central research question?
        3. Have you formulated questions to cover all aspects of your central research question?
    B. Process
        1. Has your focus changed as a result of your reading? If "yes," how?
        2. What have you learned about the pre-search stage of the research process?

SAMPLE COMMENTS FOR THE INTERPRETATION STAGE

CONTENT

1. Find articles that present opposing points of view. Compare and contrast these articles. Which viewpoint is most "in line" with your opinion on the subject? Why?
2. Can you relate this information to a personal experience?
3. Make a prediction. Based on your information, what will happen in the future? For example, if you are researching a health problem and find out it is hereditary, you can make a prediction for your future based on your family's history with the problem.
4. Can you find examples of faulty logic in your sources? Cite examples and explain the faulty logic.
5. Evaluate your source for currency, bias, and/or point of view.
6. Take a difficult passage to read and "translate" it into language we all can understand.
7. Is this information relevant? Justify your answer.
8. What information can you use to support this generalization? **OR** From these specific details, draw a conclusion.
9. Based on your information, propose a plan of action.
10. Establish criteria for making a judgment (e.g. criteria for judging scientific research or for determining child custody).
11. Suggest some solutions for a problem posed in your research. Evaluate the solutions. Prioritize the solutions. In other words, which potential solutions should be initiated first? Why?
12. Conduct an experiment to determine the validity of your hypothesis or to prove or disprove a theory proposed in one of your sources.
13. Evaluate the quantity and quality of your sources. Do you have enough sources? Do your sources represent different points of view? Are they reliable? Explain your responses.
14. How will you communicate your findings to your audience? Who is your audience? What methods of presentation will they respond to?

PROCESS

1. What obstacles have you encountered? How will you overcome them?

2. Explain your timeline for this project. Are you on schedule? Does your timeline need revision?
3. What is your next step?
4. What strategy or technique has been most successful? Why?
5. How do you feel at this stage of the process? If you feel frustrated or confused, what can you do?
6. Identify a problem you encountered and explain how you overcame it.
7. Up to this point in the research process, what have you learned about the process itself? About strategies and techniques for accomplishing steps in the process?
8. Develop criteria for judging your progress; then do a self-evaluation.
9. What can be done to improve teacher-student/librarian-student conferences? To improve peer conferences?
10. Have you made effective use of: class time, library time, and peer conferencing time? Explain. What can you do to improve your use of time? What is the first thing you will do to implement these changes?
11. Have you successfully answered your research questions? Explain.
12. Will your search continue after you finish this project? If "yes," what do you plan to do?

APPENDIX B: HOW TO READ A CHAPTER IN A TEXTBOOK OR AN ARTICLE IN A MAGAZINE USING SQ3R

1. *Survey* the chapter or article.
    a. Analyze the title.
    b. Skim the introduction and conclusion.
    c. Read information in italics or bold print.
    d. Look at pictures, charts, and/or diagrams.
    e. If a textbook chapter has questions, read the questions.
    f. If a magazine article has an abstract, read the abstract.
    g. Identify the author and consider the author's background.
    h. For an article, consider the type of magazine and the magazine's point of view.

2. Create a list of *questions* that might be answered in the chapter or article.
    a. Who?
    b. What?
    c. When?
    d. Where?
    e. Why?
    f. How?

3. *Read* the chapter or article. Try to locate the answers to the questions.

4. *Recite* the answers to the questions. Also identify information in the text that does not answer any of the questions. Should an additional question be added to the list in Step 2?

5. *Review* the questions and answers before a class discussion or test.

APPENDIX C: SAMPLE STUDENT PAPERS

Student's papers have been published as written; no changes in spelling or grammar have been made.

What Is ALS?
Sara Grunthaler
9th Grade, 1993–1994

At first I really didn't understand how to do this, but as time went on it became a lot clearer.

My first topic was psychology. I thought it was very boring, and something I wasn't interested in. I switched to allergies. I always wondered why I had them, but some of my friends didn't. I couldn't find anything in the school library, so I gave up. (Later on I found books in the town library.)

I was walking through the house looking at old pictures, when I saw a picture of my Gramma Shirley (my Dad's mother). I asked my mom what she died of, and that's how I came up with ALS (Amyotrophic Lateral Sclerosis). From that point on I was curious about what the disease does to you, how it develops, the first symptoms, and whether or not it's hereditary. The idea of ALS being hereditary played a huge role in my decision of this topic. I was really scared about whether I was going to die in my late forties. Who wouldn't be scared!? Another major factor was I wanted to find out about the disease that killed my grandmother. Whether she suffered and what she went through. I don't think I will ever stop searching for facts until they find a cure and know what causes it.

The first source I looked in was a medical book called *The Merck Manual, Twelfth Edition*. It was all scientific lingo, so I really couldn't understand it. Next, I checked out the *Funk and Wagnall's Encyclopedia*, Volume Two. I finally located some information that I understood! The only problem was that there wasn't much on ALS. I kept searching. Then I looked in two more encyclopedias (*Encyclopedia Americana*, Volume One, and *The World Book Encyclopedia*, Volume A), but they all said the same thing. I decided that since my Dad was in the medical field, maybe he knew of some new treatment. He had heard that they had located the enzyme (gene) that causes ALS. Now I *had* to find out what was going on!

I got back on InfoTrac and found some interesting articles. There was an article in *Science News*, August 21, 1993, about an enzyme called superoxide dismutase. This molecule changes into oxygen free radicals when two subunits bond. When this happens the two molecules bonded become dangerous, and then produce hydrogen peroxide or molecular oxygen. Hydrogen peroxide and molecular oxygen cause the bond to become weak and break apart. Then they steal other free radicals to make a bond again. This process only stops when there are no more radicals. "These results strongly suggest that therapy involving this enzyme or some surrogate compound (not simple antioxidants such as vitamins) may help slow both the inherited and noninherited forms of the illness," as quoted by Teepu Siddique of Northwestern University Medical School in Chicago.

ALS is a neurological disorder (neurological means having to do with the nervous system) that affects the spinal cord and lower brainstem. The motor neurons decline, and the muscles weaken and stop working. This disease usually develops in more males than females between the age of fifty to seventy years old. Most people live between eighteen months to seven years with ALS.

The hands and feet are affected first. Then it travels up to the shoulders and neck. Some people use neck braces, like my grandmother. The spinal cord and brain are damaged next. ALS patients never lose their minds, and are always able to hold their bodily wastes. The lungs are the last thing destroyed. The disease keeps slowing down the amount of motor neurons, until the lungs stop working because there aren't anymore impulses. The patient dies from lack of oxygen. It's kind of like drowning because you're not getting anymore air. I think it would be awful to die that way. My grandmother was lucky in the fact that she died in her sleep. I don't know how I would deal with it if Hanna or I got the disease. The scary thing is that I could never develop ALS, but I could pass the gene on to my children! There isn't anymore information out because they are still analyzing the disease. I hope they find out soon!

No one knows why only certain people get it, but you are more likely to develop ALS hereditarily. Scientists have many theories. One is that you are born with a faulty gene, and the disease develops later on in life. Another is that you are exposed to something that causes it. I tend to believe the second one because my grandmother had ALS, and her best friend (who lives down the street) has MS. ALS and MS are related very closely. I think that some people are born with a certain faulty gene, and when exposed to a specific chemical there is a chemical reaction. That's my theory.

I'd now like to talk about someone who I want to know more

about and would like to have met. My grandmother. Her full name was Shirley Frances Fillmore Grunthaler. My gramma was a registered nurse who worked at Christ Hospital in Jersey City. She loved to paint, and did a beautiful job. (That's where I inherited my love of painting.) She was also a Lutheran Sunday School teacher. She loved to travel, and spend time with her family. Gramma Shirley was forty-eight when diagnosed, and lived with it for three years. During those three years she had to endure a neck brace, muscle spasms, and not being able to walk (in the more advanced stage). She died in her sleep at the age of fifty-two, in February 1977.

My Dad dealt very well with losing his mother. My parents got married in July of 1978, and I was born in October. I like to think that my being born brightened my Grampa's life a little. It was kind of like when you lose someone you love, someone new comes to ease the pain. I was also the first grandchild, so I kept him pretty busy learning new things.

My Aunt Laraine had the hardest time dealing with it. My Gramma Shirley and her had been very close. She did a lot of crying, as anyone would. My aunt got over it after a while. I don't really know how my Grampa George dealt with it. I think he concentrated more on work and his kids. He did well with it. All I remember about my Great-Gramma Etta (Shirley's mother), is her saying that she always thought she would go before her only daughter did.

If I had one wish, it would be that I could have met my Gramma Shirley. We have lots of pictures of her in her younger years. Whenever I do certain things, people tell me that I act like my gramma, and that I would have liked her if I had met her. I wish I could have known what she was like, and what kind of person she was. I think she had a very fulfilling life. My Grampa George will never remarry. I was always afraid he might, and I wouldn't like my new grandmother. He's happy with his life right now.

Before I die, I hope they find a cure for ALS. The scientists are so close now, that they should find one. It's a proven fact that AIDS kills more people than ALS, but maybe if a big deal was made about ALS then the cure would be found quicker. It's not fair that all these diseases have walk-a-thons and things like that, but nobody bothers with ALS. It really makes me mad! They have treatments (not cures) for AIDS, but not even a treatment for ALS. Why is that? This disease kills people and they don't know why. AIDS can be prevented, ALS can't. When you look at it that way ALS is a lot more deadly than AIDS! I guess that by what I just wrote you can tell how I feel about the situation. When I get scared it sometimes makes me angry because people aren't trying as hard as I think they should. I think that some people besides myself feel this way also. Considering what little is known about ALS I have a right to feel this way.

BIBLIOGRAPHY

Encyclopedia Americana.
  Encyclopedia Americana Corp.; Danbury, Conn.; 1991.

Funk and Wagnall's New Encyclopedia
  Funk and Wagnall's Inc.; USA; 1992.

Merck Manual, 12th Edition
  Merck and Co.; Rahway, NJ; 1972.

World Book Encyclopedia, The
  The World Book, Inc.; USA; 1990.

Science News
  "Unstable Enzyme Underlies Inherited ALS"; August 21, 1993.

What Causes Asthma Deaths
By: Jason Inman
1993-1994

My search began when I chose a topic. First, I went to the file cabinet in the High School library, and made a list of topic ideas, which included cancer, asthma, and Alzheimer's Disease. My favorite was Asthma, since I have the disease. However, it was such a broad topic, I decided to limit it somewhat.

To narrow it down, I looked through my *Asthma Today* newsletters and found several interesting articles on Asthma Deaths. I knew this was my topic! At first, I was concerned that the information I would find might scare me a bit, and I would become overly concerned with death. After giving it a lot of consideration, I stuck with it.

I wanted to find out the causes of Asthma Deaths, and how they could be prevented. In addition, whose fault was it? Was the patient responsible or the physician?

My search began with the InfoTrac, which listed five articles that dealt with my subject. Only four were available in the library.

The first and most important article was from the *New York Times*, in the March 1993 issue. It told of a 20 year old sportsman, who died suddenly from Asthma. Doctors could do nothing to save him. He had begun using his inhaler more frequently before his death! This is a warning sign to stop and see a doctor. However, he ignored it, and paid the ultimate price.

Doctors were baffled! With all the drugs to prevent it, why were people dying? This was a mystery to me, also. Why was the death rate increasing an average of 10% a year, in the 1980's? A study during the 80's showed that Blacks and people in poverty had twice the chance of dying than whites. I believe this statistic because the poor and the disadvantaged have less accessibility to doctors and hospital care than the upper-class.

With more research, it was found that people thought Asthma was a minor inconvenience and nothing that serious. How can they say that with all the concern doctors have for this disease? But, I found out that not all doctors let their patients know how to take care of themselves. According to *Asthma Today*, one of the most common mistakes of physicians is to improperly inform the patient. Why would they do this? I would presume the more frequent the visits, the more money the doctors would make. However, I was never able to find out why! But whatever the excuse, it is a lame one!

I also found out that patients sometimes try to self-diagnose in order to avoid hospital visits, a delay which ultimately proves to be fatal. People just don't seem to realize that when you have to take more medicine, there is a problem and you must see a doctor.

Doctors usually prescribe beta-agonist-bronchodilators to the patient to open the airways. But, what doctors fail to do sometimes is to give a drug to reduce the swelling in the lungs from the attack. The bronchodilators take care of the symptoms, but not the problem. The patient believes he's okay until the problem is so severe that a hospital visit is necessary. Many other articles seem to agree with this as well.

The article then went on to blame bronchodilators for opening airways too much and allowing more Asthma causing agents in the lungs. They said if you use the drug in an allergy infested room, you might tend to stay there longer. Since you wouldn't feel bad, more damage would be caused. My doctor disagrees with that! In an interview, Dr. Frederick Oldenburg told me that in any respiratory emergency, the same drugs are pumped into the patient to open up the airways. He thinks broncodilators do not cause more problems. I tend to favor his argument because of his past track record. As far as I know, either could be right.

Another unexplainable increase is the number of Asthma cases. Up to three million kids, 18 and younger, have Asthma. I was beginning to wonder if all this wonderful polluted air we're breathing has an effect. The scientists believe so! They've done numerous studies in industrialized countries showing the same increase in Asthma. I wonder if the same thing that causes Asthma, leads to more deaths? However, none of the articles dealt with that issue.

Dr. Michael Kaliner, chief of the allergy branch at the National Institute of Allergy, says that 90% of Asthmatics have allergies. Therefore, doctors want you to remove allergens and bad air from your house to prevent serious attacks. However, that is harder than it sounds. Studies have shown that the way houses were constructed in the past ten years, they attracted the dust mite (a known trigger of Asthma). Even when you complete that task, the outdoors are full of pollutants. The outdoor pollutants should be dealt with by industrial companies, so Asthmatics can live normal lives. All the other natural allergens can be treated by specialists.

Another example of poor air making attacks worse is parental smoking. It has been proven that children with parents who smoke have worse attacks than those who don't. Most often the parents are notified by their doctors that their smoking is killing their children. However, some ignore the warning. There was a case in Maryland where a child with parents who smoked had frequent hospital visits for serious attacks. The courts warned the parents to stop smoking or lose custody of their child. The parents paid no attention to the warning, and finally the child was placed in a foster home. Who would let a young child suffer for a bad habit? The courts did the right thing in the best interest of the child.

Parents can also restrict the doctors from treating their children properly, because they want the symptoms solved. The parents force the physicians to use cough suppressants instead of broncodilators to stop the typical Asthma cough. Bronchodilators open the airways and bring up the phlegm that causes the problem. Although doctors do make mistakes, parents should allow them to do their jobs!

The *New York Times* article also mentioned that doctors have seen the error of their ways. They are beginning to recognize that beta-agonists are needed to reduce the swelling of the airways. Then, the problem, not the symptoms, needs to be treated. I don't know why their realizing this now? I have been on anti-inflammatory drugs for six years now and they're just discovering this! Either my doctor is fast or the rest of the profession is slow.

In continued research, I found that doctors believe stress is a factor in the rise in Asthma deaths. According to an article in the *Miami Herald*, a school superintendent from a New York school district, died of a massive Asthma attack only 14 months after taking over a school district with a million children. Friends and family say he was under an enormous amount of pressure. What the article failed to do was link stress and Asthma attacks. My doctor doesn't believe in stress related attacks. But, he believes that if a person thinks he/she is going to have an attack because of stress, then it will happen. I have never had a stress related attack, so I believe what my doctor said is true.

Another factor in Asthma death increases is the reaction of

viruses with medication. Steroids are often prescribed to severe Asthmatics. However, if taken when developing chicken pox, it can be deadly. A sixteen year old girl from Massachusetts died three days after coming down with the chicken pox. Her liver failed and her lungs were full of mucus. Stopping the medicine after coming down with the virus doesn't do any good. There have been cases where the organs shut down one by one, causing an agonizing death. However, there are protective measurements that can be taken before catching chicken pox to stop this. You can receive a VZIG shot (Varicella Zoster Immune Globulin) to lessen the effects of the chicken pox.

The scary part of these cases is that I almost became a statistic. In the fall of 1989, I came down with the chicken pox. A few days later, I had a bad Asthma attack, which required steroids. However, when my doctor found out I had the virus, he insisted on taking care of it some other way. He told me there was no problem, but not to use the steroids. Now that I know what could have happened, I owe my life to Dr. Oldenburg.

At this point, I was about ready to quit. I thought I had enough information to make a logical conclusion, but then I stumbled on an *Asthma Today* article on Sudden Severe Asthma Syndrome. A group of researchers from Switzerland did a study on severe Asthmatics, who had near-death cases. They formed three general groups. The first was those people who were fine and then suddenly developed an attack. These people usually deteriorated fast once brought to the hospital. The most common cause of a sudden attack is the exposure to allergens or stress.

The second group were those who would get progressively worse over days and weeks. They usually have a past history of respiratory failure and they deteriorate very fast. I could technically be placed in this group because I have slow developing attacks, but I have no prior record of any respiratory failure.

The final group is described as having "unstable or uncontrollable" Asthma. They usually develop an attack the quickest. Those who survive require a long period of time on a respirator. This group's trigger is usually a respiratory infection.

Overall, I believe that most deaths are entirely preventable, and most are the result of carelessness by patient and physician. If people just kept up with the latest medicines and used them properly, the fear of Asthma death would greatly be reduced. As for the Sudden Severe Asthma patients, I would recommend that they get a special emergency service, like "Life

Line," because you never know when a severe attack can occur. It would be nice to have some instant assistance.

I really enjoyed researching this topic because it gave me the knowledge to take care of myself!

Bibliography

Anonymous. "Asthma Deaths on the Rise In the U.S." *Jet.* October 22, 1990; p.29

——. "The Baffling Rise In Asthma Deaths." *Newsweek.* May 22, 1989; p.79

——. "Deaths From Asthma Highest in Black Areas." *Jet.* January 27, 1992; p.28

Henig, Robin M. "Asthma Kills: In Spite of Drugs." *The New York Times Magazine.* March 28, 1993; pp.42,44,50,52

Leonidas, Leo MD. (Editor) "Common Mistakes Physicians Make." *Asthma Today.* September, 1990; pp.3-4

——. "Death From Chicken Pox." *Asthma Today.* July, 1988; p.4

——. "Sudden Severe Asthma Syndrome." *Asthma Today.* February, 1991; p.3

Naunton, Ena. "Gasping For Life." *Miami Herald.* June 12, 1989; pp.1c & 2c

Oldenburg, Frederick MD. "Interview"

ANNOTATED BIBLIOGRAPHY

"Adapting the I-Search: A Potpourri of Topics and Practices." *English Journal* 78 no. 5 (September 1988): 39–45.
Presents the use of the I-Search in various subject areas such as career education and consumerism. Includes a project using the I-Search with remedial students. Practical ideas for upper elementary, middle school, and high school students.

Atwell, Nancie. *In the Middle*. Portsmouth, NH: Heinemann, 1987.
Describes Atwell's experience teaching process writing to middle school students. Provides insight into the nature of the process approach to teaching.

Bloom, Benjamin S. *Taxonomy of Educational Objectives: The Classification of Educational Goals*. New York: Longmans, Green, 1956.
Describes a hierarchy of critical thinking skills which has guided teachers and media specialists in the creation of student learning experiences and the assessment of student progress.

Breivik, Patricia Senn, and E. Gordon Gee. *Information Literacy: Revolution in the Library*. New York: American Council On Education/Macmillan, 1989.
Shows the movement from information skills to information literacy in library instruction.

California Media and Library Educators Association. *From Library Skills to Information Literacy: A Handbook for the 21st Century*. Castle Rock, CO: Hi Willow Research and Publishing, 1994.
Contains an excellent definition of information literacy.

Call, Patricia E. "SQ3R + What I Know Sheet = On Strong Strategy." *Journal of Reading* 35 no. 1 (September 1991): 50–54.
Describes how to combine SQ3R and a variation of the prenotetaking sheet to improve reading skills.

Chow, Cheryl, and Members of the Washington Library Media Association Supervisors' Subcommittee Information Skills. *Information Skills Curriculum Guide: Process, Scope, and Se-*

quence. Olympia, WA: Washington Office of the State Superintendent of Public Instruction, 1987. ERIC Document, ED 288554.
Contains the research process model adopted and modified by Maine Educational Media Association's Ad Hoc Committee on Information Skills in its *Information Skills Guide for Maine Educators* (see citation below).

Collins, Patricia J. "Bridging the Gap." *Coming to Know: Writing to Learn in the Intermediate Grades,* edited by Nancie Atwell. Portsmouth, NH: Heinemann, 1990.
Describes a process approach to teaching resource-based writing with sixth graders. Contains excellent student models.

Corbin, Richard, and Jonathan Corbin. *Research Papers: A Guided Writing Experience for Senior High School Students.* Rev. ed. New York: New York State English Council, 1978.
Presents a traditional explanation of how to write a research paper.

Dellinger, Dixie G. "Alternatives to Clip and Stitch: Real Research and Writing in the Classroom." *English Journal* 78 no. 5 (September 1988): 31–38.
Describes a collaborative learning project using the I-Search paper. Has model assignments and procedure sheets. Shows how surveys and interviews are used to gather information.

Downie, Susan L. "Ethics, a Choice for the Future: An Interdisciplinary Program." *English Journal* 78 no. 5 (September 1988): 28–30.
Focuses on using the I-Search to analyze controversial issues. Information gathering strategies include use of guest speakers, interviews with experts, and field trips.

Eisenberg, Michael B., and Michael K. Brown. "Current Themes Regarding Library and Information Instruction: Research Supporting and Research Lacking." *School Library Media Quarterly* 20 no. 2 (Winter 1992): 103–109.
Contains a summary of research findings and a list of questions for further research. Includes the following themes: the value of library and information skills instruction, the nature and scope of library and information skills, and the integrated approach. Contains comparison chart of information skills process models.

Eisenberg, Michael B., and Robert E. Berkowitz. *Information*

Problem-Solving: The Big Six Skills Approach to Library and Information Skills Instruction. Norwood, NJ: Ablex Publishing, 1993.
Describes how to implement the "Bix Six" skills across the curriculum. Another model of the research process.

Emig, Janet. *The Composing Process of Twelfth Graders.* NCTE Research Report No. 13. Urbana, IL: National Council of Teachers of English, 1971.
One of the early research studies on process writing.

Garland, Kathleen. "The Information Search Process: A Study of Elements Associated with Meaningful Research Tasks." *School Libraries Worldwide* 1 no. 1 (January 1995): 41–53.
Summarizes the results of a study investigating what makes a good research task. The five elements contributing to satisfaction with the research process and satisfaction with achievement are 1) student choice of topic, 2) group work, 3) course-related topics, 4) clarity of goals and means of evaluation, and 5) process instruction.

Irving, Ann. *Study and Information Skills Across the Curriculum.* London: Heinemann Educational Books, 1985.
Presents the philosophy behind the process approach to teaching information skills and gives one of the first models of the research process.

Joyce, Bruce, and Beverly Showers. *Student Achievement Through Staff Development: Fundamentals of School Renewal.* White Plains, NY: Longman, 1995.
Provides an understanding of staff development and its components. Useful information for planning workshops and other staff development activities.

Joyce, Marilyn Z. "The I-Search Paper: A Vehicle for Teaching the Research Process." *School Library Media Activities Monthly* 11 no. 6 (February 1995): 31–32, 37.
Provides an overview of the I-Search process.

Kaszyca, Mary, and Angela M. Krueger. "Collaborative Voices: Reflections on the I-Search Project." *English Journal* 83 no. 1 (January 1994): 62–65.
Describes an I-Search project for high school students that integrates literary research with peer support.

Kuhlthau, Carol Collier. "An Emerging Theory of Library Instruction." *School Library Media Quarterly* 16 no. 1 (Fall 1987): 23–28.
Traces the evolution of library skills instruction from the "source approach" through the "pathfinder approach" to today's "process approach."

———. "Information Search Process: A Summary of Research and Implications for School Library Media Programs." *School Library Media Quarterly* 18 no. 1 (Fall 1989): 19–25.
An explanation of Kuhlthau's model of the information search process.

———. "The Process of Learning from Information." *School Libraries Worldwide*, 1 no. 1 (January 1995): 1–12.
Presents the process approach to teaching information literacy as the key concept for the media center in the Information Age.

———. *Seeking Meaning: A Process Approach to Library and Information Services.* Norwood, NJ: Ablex Publishing, 1993.
Summarizes Kuhlthau's research resulting in her model of the Information Search Process.

Macrorie, Ken. *The I-Search Paper.* Rev. ed. Portsmouth, NH: Heinemann, 1988.
The original source of the I-Search. Proposes an alternative to the traditional research paper.

Maine Educational Media Association's Ad Hoc Committee on Information Skills. *Information Skills Guide for Maine Educators.* Augusta, ME: Maine State Library, 1990.
A curriculum guide containing the thirteen-step research process used in this book. Contains student objectives and suggests strategies for implementing stages of the research process.

Maine Educational Media Association's Information Skills Committee. *A Maine Sampler of Information Skills Activities for Maine Student Book Award Nominees, 1992–1993.* Augusta, ME: Maine State Library, 1993.
Contains a chart of Bloom's Taxonomy and corresponding action words used to generate questions and create activities for students at different levels in their thinking. The taxonomy is frequently used as an assessment tool for evaluating students' critical thinking skills.

Maxim, Donna. "Beginning Researchers." In *Coming to Know: Writing to Learn in the Intermediate Grades*, edited by Nancie Atwell. Portsmouth, NH: Heinemann, 1990.
Describes a process approach to teaching resource-based writing with third graders. Contains excellent student models.

Mitchell, Sandra Powell. "Before the Search: Genuine Communication and Literary Research." *English Journal* 78 no. 5 (September 1988): 46–49.
Applies the I-Search to an author study. Emphasizes presearch strategies and use of student journals to generate and interpret ideas.

Murray, Donald M. "Writing as a Process: How Writing Finds Its Own Meaning." In *Learning by Teaching: Selected Articles on Writing and Teaching*. Portsmouth, NH: Heinemann, 1982.
An excellent introduction to the idea of writing as information processing.

Pappas, Marjorie L. and Ann E. Tepe. *Follet Information Skills Model Kit*. McHenry, IL: Follett Software Company, 1995.

Rankin, Virginia. "One Route to Critical Thinking." *School Library Journal* 34 no. 5 (January 1988): 28–31.
Describes a process approach to research used with middle school students.

———. "Pre-Search: Intellectual Access to Information." *School Library Journal* 38 no. 3 (March 1992): 168–179.
Describes a method for teaching the presearch stage of the research process to middle school students.

———. "Rx: Task Analysis or, Relief for the Major Discomforts of Research Assignments." *School Library Journal* 38 no. 11 (November 1992): 29–32.
Suggests strategies for helping students with judging the suitability of resources, comprehending information, and evaluating and extracting information.

Stripling, Barbara K., and Judy M. Pitts. *Brainstorms and Blueprints: Teaching Library Research as a Thinking Process*. Littleton, CO: Libraries Unlimited, 1988.
Contains a model of the research process which stresses the development of critical thinking skills. Describes a variety of activities for teaching the process.

Stripling, Barbara K. "Learning-centered Libraries: Implications from Research." *School Library Media Quarterly* 23 no. 3 (Spring 1995): 163–170.
Contains an excellent section on authentic assessment.

Tadlock, Dolores Fadness. "SQ3R—Why It Works, Based on an Information Processing Theory of Learning." *Journal of Reading* 22 no. 2 (November 1978): 110–112.
Explains the reading strategy SQ3R and relates it to information processing.

Tallman, Julie I. "Helping Students to Construct Their Own Learning: The I-Search and Student-Directed Learning as a Research Experience." *Learning and Media* 23 no. 3 (1995): 10–11.
Summarizes a Maine freshman English class's experience with the I-Search.

———. "Connecting Writing and Research Through the I-Search Paper: A Teaching Partnership Between the Library Program and Classroom." *Emergency Librarian* 23 no. 1 (September-October 1995): 20–23.
A summary of the process steps used in a ninth grade I-Search experience. Contains student anecdotes.

Yanushefski, Juliana. "The Biography: The Research Project as Literary Discourse." *English Journal* 78 no. 5 (September 1988): 50–58.
Describes how to write a biography of a living person using the I-Search format.

INDEX

COLOPHON

Marilyn Z. Joyce, M.L.S., is a media specialist at Brewer High School, Brewer, Maine. She was the media specialist at Stearns High School, Millinocket, Maine, from 1988 until 1994. She has a background as a middle school and secondary English teacher prior to her taking a media specialist position.

Julie I. Tallman, Ph.D., M.L.S., is an assistant professor in the Department of Instructional Technology at The University of Georgia. She has previously taught at The University of Iowa and has previously worked as a secondary school media specialist.